FISH STEAKS AND FILLETS

83 recipes for serving up the catch of the day

by Michele Scicolone

A Particular Palate Cookbook™
Harmony Books/New York

To my husband, Charles, the best taste tester

*Special thanks to Stephen and Helen Siller, John Gillespie,
Henry Penas, and Donna and Tom Boland for their help and advice.*

A Particular Palate Cookbook

Copyright © 1988 by Michele Scicolone

Published by Harmony Books, a division of Crown Publishers, Inc.,
225 Park Avenue South, New York, New York 10003 and repre-
sented in Canada by the Canadian MANDA Group

HARMONY, PARTICULAR PALATE, and colophons are trademarks of
Crown Publishers, Inc.

Manufactured in the United States of America

Library of Congress Cataloging-in-Publication Data

Scicolone, Michele.
   Fish steaks and fillets.

    "A Particular palate cookbook."
    1. Cookery (Fish)   I. Title.
TX747.S3483   1988   641.6'92   87-12100
ISBN 0-517-56756-3

10 9 8 7 6 5 4 3

First Edition

Contents

Introduction

Eating fish is in these days. In fact, since 1980, fish consumption has risen by more than 20 percent. Experts predict that this trend will continue as more and more people realize that fresh fish is a healthy yet delicious and satisfying addition to our daily diet.

Many people prefer ordering fish in a restaurant rather than cooking it at home, because they are unsure of how to select or prepare fish. Frequently, they are confused about "new" varieties of fish that are becoming available. But fish fillets and steaks are as easy to cook as chicken parts. Perhaps even easier, since the cooking time is much shorter. They are convenient and adapt themselves to an endless variety of preparations.

In this book you will find guidelines for buying and storing fish fillets and steaks, how to cut them from a whole fish, plus detailed cooking instructions. Although each recipe suggests appropriate fish varieties, additional ideas can be found on the handy chart (page 14) that also lists alternate varieties plus descriptive information about the different species. The recipes are easy to follow and almost all of them can be prepared in less than 30 minutes. I have included some well-known classics, but most recipes are fresh, new ideas that reflect how we like to eat today. There are entire sections on microwaving, grilling, broiling, sautéing, baking, deep-frying, poaching, steaming, stewing, and braising, as well as recipes for quick toppings and sauces.

So, pick a recipe, hurry to your fish market, and start cooking a healthy, quick, and delicious meal.

Preparing Fish Steaks and Fillets

Fish fillets and fish steaks can be cut from any of hundreds of varieties of fish. Fish fillets are the sides of fish cut lengthwise away from the backbone and ribs. They are practically boneless and may or may not include the skin, depending upon the variety of fish.

Fish steaks are cross-section slices of large fish. They generally have a large central bone and are not skinned. For most cooking purposes, a fish steak should be ¾ to 1 inch thick.

The weight and size of fish steaks and fillets vary with the variety and size of the fish. When purchasing fish, figure on ¼ to ½ pound of fillets per person and ⅓ to ½ pound of steaks per person, depending on how the fish will be prepared, appetites involved, and the rest of the menu.

SELECTING FISH Appearance, odor, and texture are the three important considerations when buying fish. Whole fish should have clear, bright eyes, red-colored gills, firm flesh, and glistening skin. If possible, have the whole fish trimmed into steaks or fillets while you watch. Prepared fillets and steaks should look freshly cut, moist, and translucent. Avoid steaks with signs of sponginess or fillets that are brown near the edges. When pressed with a finger, the flesh should feel firm and elastic and spring back rapidly. Fish should always smell fresh and mild with no "fishy" odor.

At home, rinse the fish under cold water and store in airtight plastic bags. Fill a bowl with ice and place the wrapped fish on top. Refrigerate until ready to use, preferably on the same day. Oily fish tend to spoil more rapidly than lean fish. If you cannot cook them the same day, marinate the fish for a day or two.

Frozen fish is very convenient. Frozen fillets can be cooked in soups, poaches, and stews without defrosting. For breaded fish or cooking in sauce, thawing is recommended. Defrost the fish overnight in the refrigerator or under cold running water. Keep the fish in its original wrapping while it thaws.

SCALING, CLEANING, AND DRESSING A WHOLE FISH

1. Lay the fish on a work surface and grasp the tail firmly with one hand. With a fish scraper or knife held almost flat against the fish, scrape off the scales, working from tail to head. Rinse the fish thoroughly to remove loosened scales. Dry with paper towels.

2. With a sharp knife, cut the fish along the entire length of the belly. Remove the entrails and pelvic fins.

3. Remove the head and pectoral fins by cutting just behind the gills and collarbone. If the fish is large, cut the flesh through on both sides before sawing through the backbone. Remove the remaining fins by cutting along each side. Grasp the fins firmly and pull toward the head end. Use a kitchen towel on slippery fish to get a better grip.

CUTTING FISH STEAKS After the fish has been scaled, cleaned, and dressed, use a sharp, heavy knife to cut cross-section slices through the backbone, about ¾ inch thick.

FILLETING AND SKINNING FISH

1. It is not necessary to scale a fish if you plan to skin the fillets. Clean and dress the fish as above.

2. Lay the fish on a work surface with the tail end facing you. Holding the fish steady with one hand, use a sharp, flexible boning knife to cut along the backbone and over the rib bones. Cut the fillet away from the tail, leaving the tail intact. Turn the fish over and repeat. Run your fingers over the fillets to locate any remaining bones. With fingers or tweezers, carefully pull them out.

3. To skin, lay the fillet on a work surface with the tail end toward you, skin side down. Grasping the tail end firmly, make a small incision in the flesh with a sharp knife, as close

as possible to the tail end. Do not cut through the skin. Hold the knife blade flat while cutting toward the head end.

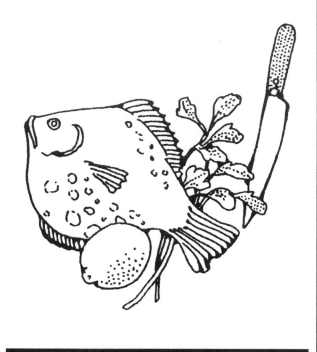

FISH NUTRITION

Calories: Low-fat fish such as cod or haddock have about 100 calories per 4-ounce serving, while high-fat fish such as salmon have about 240 calories per 4-ounce serving.

Protein: Four ounces of fish supply about half of the total amount of daily recommended protein.

Sodium: Most fish are very low in sodium with a range of from 60 to 100 milligrams per 100 grams (3½ ounces) of raw fish.

Vitamins and Minerals: Many fatty fish are high in vitamin D. Lean fish are good sources of B vitamins. Fish are also rich in minerals, including phosphorus, potassium, and iron.

A FEW WORDS ABOUT INGREDIENTS

Black and White Pepper: Throughout the ages, peppercorns have been highly prized. In ancient Rome and Greece, pepper was used as a means of paying tribute to invaders. It was so valuable in medieval times that peppercorns were often substituted for silver and gold and considered legal tender in the payment of rents, taxes, and customs duties. Pepper was bequeathed as a legacy in wills and bestowed as a dowry in marriages.

It's hard to believe that the almost tasteless powder sold today as ground pepper could be of such value. The problem is that pepper, once ground, quickly loses its flavor. For this reason, always grind pepper fresh for each use. Black pepper and white pepper are actually the same spice picked at different stages of development. Black pepper has more flavor than white pepper, but white pepper is often used in delicate sauces that would be marred by the appearance of black flecks.

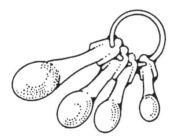

Butter: Unsalted butter is fresher and allows you to have better control of the amount of salt in a recipe. Whenever butter is called for, use unsalted or sweet butter.

Clarified Butter: Because butter contains both water and milk solids made up of protein and mineral particles, it has a tendency to burn when used for frying. For that reason, butter is often combined with a mild-flavored vegetable oil that permits the butter flavor to come through while preventing the butter from smoking at high frying temperatures.

FISH AND HEALTH

Your mother always told you that fish was good for you, but she probably never knew why. Recent studies have shown that people who consume a diet high in fish and seafood have a lower incidence of heart disease. Credit for this heart-healthy effect has been given to omega-3 fatty acids, a type of polyunsaturated fat found only in seafood and marine plants. Scientists have found that omega-3 fatty acids protect the body in three ways. They lower the level of triglycerides in the blood. High triglyceride levels have been implicated as a factor in heart disease. Omega-3 also decreases the clotting of blood, preventing blockages in coronary blood vessels. Finally, omega-3 causes blood cholesterol to drop. Some studies also suggest that omega-3 fatty acids may help to prevent breast cancer, arthritis, high blood pressure, migraine headaches, and other disorders.

Which fish provide omega-3 fatty acids? The higher the fat content of a fish, the higher its omega-3 fatty acid content. Fat content of fish varies considerably from less than 1 percent to about 15 percent, but don't be alarmed. The highest-fat fish is almost as lean as the lowest-fat red meat, so you can eat both lean and fat fish without too much concern for calories. Many doctors now recommend eating 6 ounces of fish or seafood two to three times a week. The chart on page 14 gives more information on the fat content of common fish varieties.

Clarifying eliminates the easily burned milk solids and the water content that interferes with crisping. To clarify, slowly melt the butter in a small saucepan over very low heat. Remove from heat and allow to cool several minutes. With a spoon, skim off the foam that rises to the surface. Carefully pour the clear golden liquid into a storage container, discarding the milky residue. One stick of butter yields about 6 tablespoons of clarified butter. The clarified butter may be used immediately or stored in the refrigerator or freezer up to one month.

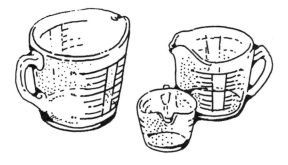

Oil: Olive oil is the oil I use most frequently. For sautéing, I use a "pure" olive oil, relatively light and mild in flavor. For dressings and sauces where a more definite olive flavor is desired, I use an extra-virgin olive oil from Italy. There are many good brands of olive oil on the market. Taste several brands until you find one you like. Remember that olive oil is perishable and should be stored in a cool dark place. Don't buy more olive oil than you can use in a relatively short time.

For deep-frying and recipes where a more neutral flavor is desired I prefer corn oil. Peanut oil is also a good choice for frying. Its flavor is especially complementary to Oriental cuisine.

Parsley: Parsley is the one fresh herb that I always keep on hand. Its flavor is good with fish steaks and fillets and it adds a touch of freshness to all foods. Used in combination with dried herbs such as tarragon or basil, fresh parsley seems to bring them to life, restoring some of their original flavor. Dried parsley, however, is so lacking in flavor as to be practically useless.

There are two types of fresh parsley commonly available, flat leaf and curly leaf. Flat-leaf parsley, sometimes called Italian parsley, is more flavorful, though curly parsley is more decorative. Whichever you prefer, fresh parsley can be kept easily for a week to ten days in the refrigerator. Trim the base of the stems and place the parsley in a jar with 2 inches of water. Cover the parsley with a plastic bag and refrigerate. Change the water every two days and the parsley will remain fresh.

A FEW WORDS ABOUT EQUIPMENT
Wide Slotted Spatula or Pancake Turner:

For handling delicate fish fillets and steaks, this tool is invaluable. Look for spatulas, either metal or plastic, with a surface at least 4 inches wide to facilitate turning fillets or transferring them from pan to serving plate.

Hinged Wire Basket: No matter how well-greased the grill, barbecued fillets and steaks tend to stick to the hot metal and break apart when you try to turn them over. A hinged wire basket can eliminate this problem since not only the fish but the basket itself is turned. Some wire baskets are made with a nonstick coating that further helps to prevent sticking. The only drawback is that since the fish are not seared by the hot grill, they do not acquire the grid marks that make grilled foods so attractive. To ensure grid marks, preheat the wire basket 10 to 15 minutes before adding fish.

The best type of basket is one that can be adjusted to the thickness of the food. At least one manufacturer makes a basket specifically made for fillets with fish-shaped grooves, but I have yet to find a fillet that fits the grooves and prefer an all-purpose basket.

EATING RAW FISH—THE PROS AND CONS

Prompted by health and diet concerns, the fashion for eating raw fish, especially in the form of sushi and sashimi, continues to grow. But eating raw fish brings increased health risks because fish, like any other living creature, can carry bacteria and parasites.

All freshwater fish, such as salmon, and a few varieties of in-shore or migrating saltwater fish, such as mackerel, eel, and herring, are susceptible to parasites. If the fish are eaten raw, these parasites may cause illness, and eating any of these varieties raw is not recommended.

Saltwater fish are generally safe to eat raw, although certain varieties such as cod, haddock, or whiting, which are caught close to shore, are occasionally found to contain worms. Fish processors routinely "candle" fillets, that is, the fillets are held over a light to detect the presence of any worms before the fish are sent to market, but sometimes one does slip through. These worms, while not esthetic, are harmless and are destroyed by cooking.

Raw fish selected and prepared by an experienced sushi chef are not likely to cause problems. The chef has been trained to choose the right varieties for sushi and knows how to handle them to keep them fresh and avoid contamination from other foods. So if you like your fish raw, make it a rule to eat only fish selected and prepared by an expert.

FISH STEAKS AND FILLETS AVAILABLE AND SUBSTITUTIONS

"There are more than 20,000 kinds of fish, as many as amphibians, reptiles, birds, and mammals added together; most of them are edible," wrote Waverly Root in *Food*. What's more, many fish varieties go by different names in different locations, so it's not hard to be confused about choosing fish. But your local fish market probably stocks no more than a few varieties with which you can quickly become familiar. Ask for recommendations and don't hesitate to experiment. When in doubt, consult the following chart, which lists some of the more readily available varieties and alternate possibilities.

Variety	Fillets or Steaks	Consistency	Fat or Lean	Substitute
Bluefish	Fillets	Fine	Fat	Mullet, Trout, Mackerel
Butterfish	Fillets	Fine	Fat	Sole, Pompano, Porgy
Catfish	Both	Firm	Lean	Whitefish, Sole, Perch
Cod (Scrod)	Both	Firm	Lean	Haddock, Pollack, Pike, Hake
Croaker	Fillets	Firm	Lean	Cod, Cusk, Drum
Flounder	Fillets	Fine	Lean	Sole, Whiting, Whitefish
Grouper	Both	Firm	Lean	Monkfish, Tilefish, Sea Bass
Haddock	Fillets	Firm	Lean	Cod, Pollack, Whitefish
Halibut	Steaks	Firm	Lean	Tilefish, Sea Bass, Cod
Mackerel	Fillets	Firm	Fat	Bluefish, Kingfish, Swordfish
Monkfish	Fillets	Firm	Lean	Grouper, Tilefish, Halibut
Mullet	Fillets	Firm	Moderate	Bluefish, Mackerel, Pompano
Orange Roughy	Fillets	Firm	Lean	Cod, Sole, Sea Bass

Variety	Fillets or Steaks	Consistency	Fat or Lean	Substitute
Perch	Fillets	Firm	Lean	Sea Bass, Flounder
Pike	Fillets	Firm	Lean	Cod, Orange Roughy, Sole
Pollack	Fillets	Firm	Moderate	Cod, Bluefish, Pike
Pompano	Fillets	Firm	Moderate	Butterfish, Sole
Porgy	Fillets	Firm	Lean	Sole, Butterfish, Perch
Redfish	Fillets	Firm	Lean	Croaker, Drum, Flounder
Red Snapper	Fillets	Firm	Lean	Sea Bass, Sea Trout, Sole
Rockfish	Fillets	Firm	Lean	Perch, Red Snapper
Salmon	Both	Firm	Moderate to Fat	Swordfish, Tuna, Shark
Sea Bass	Both	Firm	Lean	Orange Roughy, Sea Trout
Shad	Fillets	Firm	Fat	Butterfish, Flounder
Shark	Steaks	Firm	Lean	Salmon, Swordfish, Tuna
Sole	Fillets	Fine	Lean	Flounder, Whitefish
Striped Bass	Fillets	Fine	Fat	Red Snapper, Sea Bass, Sole
Swordfish	Steaks	Firm	Moderate	Shark, Tuna, Salmon
Tilefish	Steaks	Firm	Lean	Halibut, Rockfish, Monkfish
Trout	Fillets	Firm	Fat	Salmon, Pike
Tuna	Steaks	Firm	Moderate	Salmon, Swordfish, Shark
Turbot	Fillets	Fine	Lean	Flounder, Sole, Whiting
Weakfish	Fillets	Firm	Lean	Sea Bass, Cod, Haddock
Whitefish	Both	Firm	Moderate	Trout, Pike, Cod
Whiting	Fillets	Firm	Lean	Flounder, Whitefish, Sole

Grilling and Broiling

"Take an old grill, three feet high, twisted
by ancient fires, lay the fish upon it,
baptize it with the sauce, and plant the
whole thing in the middle of your fiery
inferno."

Colette
Prisons et Paradis

Fish steaks and fillets acquire a special smoky flavor when cooked on a hot grill. Thick steaks and firm fillets fare best on the barbecue, but thinner fillets and steaks can be grilled if you use a hinged grilling basket. Thoroughly preheat the grill before cooking, then brush the grill racks with oil before adding fish. Watch fish carefully since it cooks very quickly. Baste it frequently to prevent drying out. Keep in mind that outdoor temperature, size, and hotness of the fire will affect cooking time.

Nothing could be simpler or quicker than broiled fish fillets or steaks. Always preheat the broiler and broiler pan, and brush the pan with butter or oil. Add the steaks or fillets and brush them lightly with marinade, basting sauce, butter, or oil to maintain moistness. Arrange the broiler pan close to the heat source for thin pieces of fish and farther away for thicker pieces. For instance, a ¼-inch-thick fillet can be placed 2 inches from the source of heat while a ¾-inch-thick piece should be placed 4 inches away. Thin pieces do not need to be turned during cooking and thicker pieces should be turned only once.

FISH STEAKS with PESTO

4 servings

Pesto

1 cup fresh basil leaves
1 large garlic clove, peeled
2 tablespoons pine nuts or almonds
½ cup olive oil
Salt and pepper to taste

4 salmon, swordfish, or tuna steaks, about
    ¾ inch thick
2 tablespoons olive oil

1. In a food processor or blender, process the basil, garlic, and nuts until finely chopped. Gradually blend in the oil. Add salt and pepper to taste.

2. Prepare the grill or preheat the broiler. Brush the steaks with oil and sprinkle with salt and pepper. Grill or broil the fish for 3 minutes on each side. Serve hot or at room temperature with the pesto.

SALMON

At one time, salmon was so cheap and plentiful that servants demanded—and received—a contract stating that they would not be required to eat salmon more than three times a week! Today, salmon is one of the most popular fish, much as it was in A.D. 77 when the Roman scholar Pliny wrote: "the river salmon is preferred to all fish that swim the sea."

In general, the redder the color of the salmon flesh, the tastier it is. The varieties with the highest fat content, usually about 12 to 16 percent, are considered more desirable. Six varieties of salmon are commonly found in North American markets, only one of which is from the Atlantic Ocean. They are:

Atlantic Salmon: With pink to orange flesh, this variety has a high fat content of 12 percent or more. Much of it comes from fish farms in Canada and Norway.

Chinook Salmon: The largest of the Pacific salmon, chinook is often called king salmon. With a fat content of about 15 percent at its prime, this is also the richest of the varieties.

Sockeye Salmon: Also called red salmon, this variety has a fat content of about 9 percent. Although some is sold fresh, it is considered the prime variety for canning.

Coho or Silver Salmon: With a deep salmon-colored flesh, it is the favorite salmon for smoking.

Pink Salmon: The most common variety with a low fat content. Much pink salmon is canned.

Chum Salmon: With pale-colored flesh and the lowest fat content, at about 5 percent, most chum salmon is used for canning, although it is often fished for its roe, which is eaten as caviar.

GRILLED SALMON FAJITAS

Fajitas are usually made with strips of marinated skirt steak but salmon is a delicious change, particularly when grilled over mesquite. This recipe makes a generous amount of guacamole, so have some tortilla chips on hand for dipping.

4–6 servings

Marinade
¼ cup fresh lime juice
2 tablespoons salad oil
2 tablespoons chopped chilies
2 tablespoons tequila (optional)

1½ pounds skinless salmon fillets

Guacamole
2 medium ripe avocados
2 tablespoons lime juice
½ teaspoon salt
1 medium ripe tomato, seeded and chopped
¼ cup finely chopped sweet onion
2 tablespoons chopped fresh coriander
2 tablespoons minced hot chilies or to taste

Salsa
1 medium ripe tomato, diced
¼ cup finely chopped sweet onion
1 to 2 tablespoons minced hot chilies
2 tablespoons chopped fresh coriander
¼ teaspoon salt

Warm flour tortillas
Sour cream

1. In a shallow glass or stainless steel bowl, combine lime juice, salad oil, chilies, and tequila. Add the salmon, cover, and refrigerate for 2 hours, turning occasionally.

2. To prepare the guacamole, coarsely mash the avocados with the lime juice and salt in a stainless steel or glass bowl. Stir in the remaining ingredients. Taste for seasoning.

3. To prepare the salsa, combine all ingredients in a glass or stainless steel bowl.

4. Prepare the grill or preheat the broiler. Grill the salmon for 2 to 3 minutes on each side. Transfer to a cutting board and slice thinly.

5. To assemble, place a warm flour tortilla on plate; put some salmon slices down the center of the tortilla. Top with guacamole, salsa, and sour cream. Fold the sides of the tortilla over the filling.

SICILIAN STUFFED SWORDFISH ROLLS

Some of the best swordfish I have ever tasted was on the island of Sicily. This recipe was given to me by a lady in Taormina, a most beautiful town in the shadow of Mount Etna.

4 servings

4 swordfish, tuna, or shark steaks, ½ inch thick
½ cup fresh bread crumbs
½ cup chopped and seeded ripe tomato
2 tablespoons chopped parsley
1 large garlic clove, crushed
½ teaspoon dried oregano
½ teaspoon salt
¼ teaspoon freshly ground black pepper
4 tablespoons olive oil
2 tablespoons lemon juice

1. Prepare the grill or preheat the broiler.

2. Place the fish steaks between two sheets of plastic wrap, and gently pound each piece to ¼-inch thickness.

3. In a medium bowl, combine the bread crumbs, tomato, parsley, garlic, oregano, salt, pepper, and 2 tablespoons olive oil. Place about 2 tablespoons of the mixture on one end of each steak. Roll up the steaks and secure with wooden picks.

4. Combine the remaining olive oil and lemon juice. Brush over fish rolls. Broil or grill the fish for 2 minutes on each side.

"Only eat fish and ripened rice."
Chinese proverb

TERIYAKI FISH STEAKS

4 servings

Marinade

⅓ cup soy sauce
¼ cup dry sherry
1 tablespoon sugar
2 tablespoons peeled and grated fresh ginger-
    root
1 garlic clove, crushed

4 swordfish, tuna, or salmon steaks, about
    ¾ inch thick

1. In a shallow dish combine the marinade ingredients. Add the fish steaks. Cover and refrigerate for 2 hours, turning occasionally.

2. Prepare the grill or preheat the broiler. Grill or broil the fish for 2 to 3 minutes on each side. Baste with the marinade several times during the cooking.

DAD'S GRILLED BLUEFISH

My father loved to go fishing. Sometimes his catch was meager, but usually he brought home more fish than we could eat, which he would share with our neighbors. This is his favorite way to prepare bluefish.

4–6 servings

Marinade

⅓ cup olive oil
⅓ cup red wine vinegar
¼ cup chopped fresh mint leaves
2 large garlic cloves, finely chopped
½ teaspoon salt
¼ teaspoon pepper

1 ½ pounds bluefish or mackerel fillets

1. Whisk together the marinade ingredients. Put the fillets in a shallow glass or stainless steel dish; pour on marinade. Cover and refrigerate several hours or overnight, turning occasionally.

2. Prepare the grill or preheat the broiler. Pour marinade into a small saucepan and place on the grill or stove to heat. Grill or broil the fish for 4 to 5 minutes on each side, basting frequently with marinade. Serve with the remaining marinade.

GRILLED SWORDFISH with FRESH TOMATO SAUCE

4 servings

Sauce

1 pound firm, ripe tomatoes, seeded and
    diced
½ cup Greek black olives, pitted and sliced
¼ cup finely chopped fresh basil
1 small garlic clove, minced
½ teaspoon salt
¼ teaspoon pepper
¼ cup olive oil

4 swordfish, tuna, or shark steaks, about
    ¾ inch thick
2 tablespoons olive oil
Salt and pepper to taste

1. In a large bowl, combine the sauce ingredients. Cover and let stand at room temperature for 1 hour.

2. Prepare the grill or preheat the broiler. Brush the steaks with oil and sprinkle with salt and pepper to taste. Grill for 2 to 3 minutes on each side. Serve with the tomato sauce.

GRILLED TUNA STEAKS with MANGO SALSA

Marie Simmons is a cookbook author, magazine food writer, and one of the most creative cooks I know. Marie says, "This pretty yellow salsa is indeed summer fare; mangoes, limes, and fresh herbs all being easily obtainable only in the warmer months of the year. But the fish steaks can be broiled, and if mangoes are unavailable, substitute fresh or canned unsweetened pineapple."

4 servings

Mango Salsa
2 tablespoons mild olive or other vegetable oil
1 tablespoon fresh lime juice
1 small garlic clove, crushed
¼ teaspoon salt
1 large ripe mango, peeled and cut into
    ¼-inch dice (about 1½ cups)
2 tablespoons each diced sweet red and white
    onions
1 scallion, including top, sliced thinly on the
    diagonal
1 tablespoon chopped fresh basil leaves, including stems
1 teaspoon chopped fresh mint
1 teaspoon minced hot chili (or more to taste)

4 tuna, swordfish, or shark steaks, about
    ¾ inch thick
2 teaspoons mild olive or other vegetable oil
Salt
Lime wedges

1. In a medium bowl, whisk together the oil, lime juice, garlic, and salt. Add the mango, red and white onions, scallion, basil, mint, and chili; toss gently. Cover and set aside at room temperature until ready to serve.

2. Prepare the grill or preheat the broiler.

3. Brush the surface of the fish lightly with oil. Sprinkle with salt. Grill or broil 4 to 5 inches from the heat source, until lightly browned, about 3 to 4 minutes on each side. The steaks should be just barely pink in the center. Garnish with lime wedges and serve with mango salsa.

GRILLED TUNA BALSAMICO

Balsamic vinegar is a dark red, slightly sweet wine vinegar from Italy. The unique flavor of balsamic vinegar comes from the five different kinds of wood barrels in which it ages. The best balsamic vinegars are aged a minimum of seven years although older vintages can be 100 years old. Of course, these are very rare. They are believed to have health-giving properties and are often used for medicinal purposes.

4 servings

Marinade
⅓ cup balsamic vinegar
⅓ cup olive oil
¼ cup minced fresh parsley
2 large garlic cloves, crushed
½ teaspoon salt
¼ teaspoon pepper

4 tuna, swordfish, or shark steaks, ¾ inch thick
1 large eggplant, cut crosswise into ½-inch slices
Salt
1 red pepper, halved lengthwise and seeded
1 yellow pepper, halved lengthwise and seeded
2 small sweet onions, cut in half

1. Whisk together the marinade ingredients. Put the steaks in a shallow glass or stainless steel dish; pour on marinade. Cover and refrigerate for 2 to 4 hours, turning the steaks occasionally.

2. Sprinkle the eggplant slices with salt; let them stand in a colander for 30 minutes. Wipe with paper towels.

3. Prepare the grill or preheat the broiler. Brush the eggplant, peppers, and onions with the marinade. Grill or broil the vegetables for 5 minutes, or until browned. With a wide spatula, turn the vegetables. Add the steaks and grill for 2 minutes on each side, basting with the marinade.

SALMON AU POIVRE

Crushed peppercorns form a delicious crust on grilled fish steaks. To crush the peppercorns, use a mortar and pestle or place them in a bag and crush them gently with a skillet.

4 servings

3 tablespoons softened butter
1 tablespoon chopped mixed herbs (fresh parsley, fresh or dried thyme, tarragon, chives, or basil)
4 salmon, swordfish, or tuna steaks, about ¾ inch thick
Salt
2 tablespoons crushed peppercorns (use all black or a mixture of black, white, brown, and green)

1. In a small bowl, combine the butter and herbs. Set aside.

2. Prepare the grill or preheat the broiler. Sprinkle the fish with salt. Scatter the peppercorns on a sheet of wax paper. With the heel of your hand, press the peppercorns into the fish. Broil or grill for 2 to 3 minutes on each side. Top with the herb butter.

GRILLED SWORDFISH with MUSTARD SAUCE

4 servings

Sauce
1 tablespoon butter
2 tablespoons finely chopped scallions
⅓ cup dry white wine
½ cup heavy cream
¼ cup Dijon-style mustard

4 swordfish, salmon, shark, or tuna steaks, about ¾ inch thick
Salt
Black pepper
Worcestershire sauce

1. Prepare the grill or preheat the broiler.

2. In a small saucepan, melt the butter and sauté the scallions until tender, about 3 minutes. Add the wine and cook until most of the liquid is evaporated. Stir in the heavy cream. Simmer until slightly thickened, about 1 minute. Beat in the mustard. Remove from heat, cover, and keep warm while grilling the fish.

3. Sprinkle the fish steaks with salt, pepper, and a few drops of Worcestershire. Grill or broil the fish for 2 to 3 minutes on each side. Spoon the sauce onto plates, and top with the fish steaks.

HOISIN GRILLED SWORDFISH

6 servings

Marinade
3 tablespoons hoisin sauce
2 tablespoons dry sherry
2 tablespoons rice wine vinegar
1 tablespoon Oriental sesame oil
2 tablespoons chopped scallions
1 large garlic clove, finely chopped
1 teaspoon peeled and grated fresh gingerroot

6 swordfish, tuna, shark, cod, or tilefish steaks, about ¾ inch thick

1. In a small bowl, combine the hoisin sauce, sherry, vinegar, sesame oil, scallions, garlic, and gingerroot. Place the fish in a shallow dish and spread with the hoisin mixture. Cover and refrigerate for at least 1 hour.

2. Prepare the grill or preheat the broiler. Broil or grill the fish for 3 to 4 minutes on each side.

SHARK STEAKS with PEPPERS AND ANCHOVIES

The first time I tasted shark, I thought that the chef had made a mistake and substituted veal. Despite its bad reputation, shark is a delicious fish.

4 servings

4 shark, tuna, or swordfish steaks, about
    ¾ inch thick
3 tablespoons lemon juice
4 tablespoons olive oil
1 teaspoon oregano
Salt and black pepper
3 garlic cloves, finely chopped
1 can (2 ounces) flat anchovy fillets, drained
4 red peppers, seeded and thinly sliced

1. In a shallow dish, sprinkle the fish with lemon juice, 2 tablespoons olive oil, ½ teaspoon oregano, and salt and pepper to taste. Cover and refrigerate for 1 hour.

2. In a large skillet, heat the remaining olive oil over medium heat. Add the garlic and sauté for 30 seconds. Stir in the anchovy fillets. Add the peppers, remaining oregano, and salt and pepper to taste. Cover and cook for 15 to 20 minutes, stirring frequently, until the peppers are tender. Uncover and raise the heat; cook until the liquid is evaporated, about 3 minutes.

3. Prepare the grill or preheat the broiler. Grill or broil the fish steaks for 2 to 3 minutes on each side. Serve with the sautéed peppers and anchovies.

"Fish and guests grow stale in three days."
Chinese proverb

BARBECUED SHARK

A tangy barbecue sauce is just as good on fresh fish as it is on chicken or beef.

6 servings

Sauce
2 tablespoons butter
1 medium onion, finely chopped
1 garlic clove, minced
½ cup catsup
½ cup orange juice
3 tablespoons red wine vinegar
3 tablespoons brown sugar
1 teaspoon Worcestershire sauce

6 shark, swordfish, or tilefish steaks

1. In a medium saucepan, melt the butter. Add the onion and sauté until tender, about 5 minutes. Stir in the remaining ingredients except for the fish. Bring to a simmer and cook, stirring occasionally for 10 to 15 minutes, or until thickened.

2. Prepare the grill or preheat the broiler. Brush the fish with the sauce. Grill or broil the fish for 2 to 3 minutes on each side, basting frequently.

HERBED FISH KEBABS

4–6 servings

Marinade
½ cup olive oil
¼ cup lemon juice
1 tablespoon Worcestershire sauce
1 large garlic clove, chopped
½ teaspoon dried thyme
½ teaspoon dried marjoram
Salt and black pepper to taste

1½ pounds shark, swordfish, or halibut
    steaks, about 1 inch thick
1 small red onion, quartered
1 cup cherry tomatoes
1 green pepper, cut into 1-inch cubes
4 ounces small mushrooms

1. In a shallow bowl, combine the oil, lemon juice, Worcestershire, garlic, thyme, marjoram, and salt and pepper to taste.

2. Cut the fish into 1-inch chunks, trimming away the skin and bones. Combine the fish with the marinade ingredients. Cover and chill several hours or overnight.

3. Prepare the grill or preheat the broiler. Alternately thread the fish and vegetables onto 6 skewers. Grill or broil the fish, basting with the marinade, for 3 minutes on each side.

GRILLED TUNA with TOMATO CHILI SALSA

6 servings

Marinade
½ cup olive oil
4 tablespoons lime juice
4 garlic cloves, chopped
¼ cup finely chopped coriander or parsley
½ teaspoon salt
¼ teaspoon pepper

6 tuna, swordfish, or shark steaks, or thick
    fish fillets

Salsa
2 tablespoons butter
¼ cup chopped scallions
1 or 2 small hot chilies, seeded and chopped
4 garlic cloves, minced
3 large tomatoes, peeled, seeded, and chopped
1 tablespoon lime juice
½ teaspoon salt
¼ teaspoon pepper
¼ cup chopped fresh coriander or parsley

1. In a large shallow dish, combine the marinade ingredients. Add the fish, and cover and chill for several hours or overnight, turning occasionally.

2. In a medium saucepan, melt the butter. Add the scallions, chilies, and garlic, and sauté for 3 to 4 minutes. Add the tomatoes, lime juice, salt, and pepper. Bring to a simmer and cook for 10 minutes, stirring occasionally. Remove from the heat, and stir in the coriander.

3. Prepare the grill or preheat the broiler. Grill or broil the fish for 3 to 4 minutes on each side, basting occasionally with the marinade. Serve with the salsa.

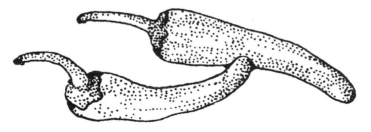

TANDOORI SWORDFISH

A *tandoor* is a circular Indian oven that cooks with intense heat, leaving foods crusty on the outside but moist on the inside. The spicy yogurt marinade is typical for foods to be cooked in a tandoor.

6 servings

Marinade
½ teaspoon ground coriander
¼ teaspoon freshly ground white pepper
½ teaspoon ground cumin
¼ teaspoon ground turmeric
2 garlic cloves, crushed
8 ounces plain yogurt
1 teaspoon salt
1 teaspoon peeled and grated fresh gingerroot
Pinch cayenne

6 swordfish, salmon, or shark steaks, about
    ¾ inch thick
1 lime, cut into wedges

1. In a small bowl, combine the marinade ingredients. Cover and refrigerate overnight.

2. Pour the marinade over the fish, and let stand for 30 minutes.

3. Prepare the grill or preheat the broiler. Scrape most of the marinade off the fish. Grill or broil the fish for 2 minutes on each side. Serve with lime wedges.

GREEK TUNA SALAD

4 servings

Dressing

½ cup olive oil
3 tablespoons fresh lemon juice
1 tablespoon Dijon-style mustard
1 large garlic clove, crushed
1 teaspoon oregano
¼ teaspoon salt
⅛ teaspoon pepper

4 tuna, swordfish, or shark steaks, about
    ¾ inch thick
6 cups torn leaf lettuce
1 small red onion, thinly sliced
4 ounces feta cheese, cut into ½-inch dice
1 large ripe tomato, cut into wedges
½ cup Greek-style black olives

1. In a small bowl, whisk together the dressing ingredients.

2. Arrange the fish in a shallow dish, and drizzle with ⅓ cup of the dressing. Cover and marinate in refrigerator for 1 hour.

3. Prepare the grill or preheat the broiler. Grill or broil the steaks for 2 to 3 minutes on each side, basting with the marinade.

4. In a large bowl toss the lettuce, onion, cheese, tomato, and olives together with the remaining dressing. Arrange the salad on four plates, and top with the fish steaks.

TUNA with SESAME-GINGER SAUCE

This spicy sauce is delicious on all kinds of fish steaks. Spoon left over sauce over a green salad, chilled asparagus, or green beans.

6 servings

Sauce
⅓ cup olive oil
⅓ cup rice wine vinegar
2 tablespoons lemon juice
2 tablespoons soy sauce
1 to 2 teaspoons Oriental sesame oil
½ teaspoon sugar
⅛ teaspoon freshly ground pepper
¼ cup toasted sesame seeds (see note)
¼ cup finely chopped coriander
2 tablespoons finely chopped scallion
1 tablespoon peeled and grated fresh ginger-root

6 tuna, swordfish, or salmon steaks, about ¾ inch thick
1 tablespoon olive oil
Salt and pepper

1. In a small bowl, whisk together the oil, vinegar, lemon juice, soy sauce, sesame oil, sugar, and pepper. Stir in the remaining sauce ingredients.

2. Prepare the grill or preheat the broiler. Brush the fish steaks with oil; sprinkle with salt and pepper. Grill for 2 to 3 minutes on each side, and serve with sesame-ginger sauce.

Note: To toast sesame seeds, spread the seeds in a jelly roll pan. Bake for 10 minutes in a preheated 350°F. oven, stirring occasionally.

Sautéing and Stir-frying

"They fried the fish with bacon and were astonished; for no fish had ever seemed so delicious before."

Mark Twain

When properly prepared, sautéed fish fillets have a crisp, golden exterior and a tender, moist interior. Butter gives the best flavor to sautéed fish, but, since it burns easily, it is best to use either clarified butter or a combination of butter and oil. Olive oil is also a good choice.

Choose a heavy sauté pan or skillet large enough to hold the fish without crowding them, or cook the fish in small batches. Sauté the bone side of a fillet first so that it will be face up when it is served.

The secret to successful stir-frying is to have all the ingredients chopped, sliced, and ready to use before starting to cook. It's important to use firm-textured fish when stir-frying so that it will not crumble. Although the Chinese use a wok, a large heavy skillet can be substituted.

SAUTEED SOLE with BASIL AND GARLIC

4-6 servings

½ cup flour
½ teaspoon salt
⅛ teaspoon pepper
1½ pounds sole, snapper, or whitefish fillets,
    cut into serving pieces
3 tablespoons butter
2 tablespoons olive oil
1 garlic clove, minced
¼ cup chopped fresh basil
1 tablespoon lemon juice

1. On a piece of wax paper, combine the flour, salt, and pepper. Dip the fillets in the flour mixture; shake to remove excess.

2. In a large heavy skillet, melt 2 tablespoons butter with the oil over medium heat. Add the fish fillets and sauté until golden brown, about 2 minutes on each side. Remove the fish to a warm serving platter.

3. Add the garlic to the skillet. Sauté for 30 seconds. Remove from heat; stir in basil, remaining butter, and lemon juice. Pour over the fish and serve.

TUNA with SWEET AND SOUR ONIONS

4 servings

¼ cup olive oil
4 tuna, swordfish, or shark steaks, about
    ¾ inch thick
Salt and pepper to taste
2 cups sliced onions
⅓ cup white wine vinegar
2 teaspoons sugar
¼ cup chopped fresh mint leaves
¼ teaspoon salt
⅛ teaspoon pepper

1. In a large skillet, heat the oil over medium heat. Add the fish and sauté for 2 minutes on each side. Remove to a warm platter with a slotted spatula. Sprinkle with salt and pepper to taste.

2. In the same skillet, sauté the onions over medium-low heat until very tender and brown, about 10 minutes. Stir in the vinegar, sugar, mint, salt, and pepper. Cover and cook for an additional 5 minutes.

3. Return the fish to the skillet. Baste with the onion sauce, and cook 3 to 5 minutes longer.

FISH BURGERS with CHILI-TARTAR SAUCE

Even non-fish eaters will love these tasty fish cakes. They're terrific hot, but they are also delicious when served cold on a roll with lettuce and tomato topped with chili-tartar sauce. Miniature fish burgers make wonderful party appetizers.

4–6 servings

Chili-Tartar Sauce
½ cup mayonnaise
¼ cup sour cream
1 to 2 tablespoons chopped hot chilies
1 teaspoon chili powder
1 large garlic clove

1 pound flounder, sole, or perch fillets, finely
    chopped
1½ cups fresh bread crumbs
1 egg plus 1 egg yolk
¼ cup finely chopped scallions
¼ cup finely chopped red or green pepper
¼ cup mayonnaise
1 tablespoon fresh lemon juice
½ teaspoon dry mustard
Dash hot pepper sauce
1 teaspoon salt
⅛ teaspoon cayenne pepper
3 tablespoons butter
3 tablespoons vegetable oil

1. In a food processor or blender, combine the sauce ingredients. Blend or process until smooth. Scrape into a small container. Cover and chill several hours or overnight.

2. In a large bowl, combine the fish, ½ cup bread crumbs, egg and yolk, scallions, pepper, mayonnaise, lemon juice, mustard, hot pepper sauce, salt, and cayenne pepper. Toss lightly to blend.

3. Spread the remaining bread crumbs on wax paper. Divide the fish mixture into eight portions and shape into patties, about ¾ inch thick. Coat with the bread crumbs. Place the fish cakes on a rack over a plate in the refrigerator, and chill for 1 hour.

4. In a large heavy skillet over medium heat, melt the butter with the oil. Add the fish burgers and sauté for 4 to 5 minutes on each side, or until browned and firm when pressed in the center. Serve with the chili-tartar sauce.

"The fact is I simply adore fish,
   But I don't know a perch from a pike;
   And I can't tell a cray from a crawfish
   They look and they taste so alike."
                                    William Cole

WARM SALMON SALAD

A beautiful warm salad with Japanese overtones.

4 servings

4 ounces spinach, trimmed
1 endive, separated into leaves
1 bunch watercress, stems trimmed
1 pound salmon fillet, skinned
¼ cup vegetable oil
½ cup sliced scallions
1 tablespoon peeled and grated fresh ginger-
    root
3 tablespoons lemon juice
2 tablespoons Japanese soy sauce
¼ cup mixed chopped fresh herbs such as
    parsley, dill, chives, basil, or thyme

1. Tear the spinach leaves into bite-size pieces and arrange on four plates. Top with the endive and watercress.

2. Slice the salmon into ½-inch-thick slices. Cut each slice into 1-inch pieces.

3. In a large nonstick skillet, heat the oil over medium heat. Add the salmon pieces and sauté for 1 minute. Stir in the scallions and gingerroot, and sauté for 30 seconds more. Add the lemon juice and soy sauce, and bring to a simmer. Remove from heat; stir in herbs. Spoon the salmon and sauce over the greens, and serve.

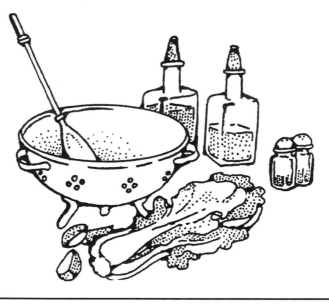

TUNA STEAKS with RED WINE SAUCE

In this recipe the fish steaks are cooked quickly in a very hot pan to brown the outside while the inside remains rare. The color, flavor, and texture resemble beef and the red wine sauce is a delicious complement.

4 servings

Sauce

3 tablespoons minced shallots
1 garlic clove, minced
⅓ cup dry red wine
⅓ cup red wine vinegar
2 sticks (8 ounces) butter, cut into ½-inch-thick pieces
¼ teaspoon salt
⅛ teaspoon pepper

2 teaspoons vegetable oil
4 tuna or swordfish steaks, about ½ inch thick
Salt and black pepper to taste

1. In a small saucepan, combine the shallots, garlic, wine, and vinegar over medium heat. Boil until the liquid is reduced to 2 tablespoons. Reduce heat to very low. With a whisk, beat in the butter one piece at a time, until sauce is smooth and creamy. Remove from heat, cover, and keep warm. Do not reheat or sauce will separate.

2. Heat a large nonstick skillet over medium high heat until hot enough to evaporate a drop of water on contact. Brush the skillet with oil. Add the tuna steaks and sauté until lightly browned, about 2 minutes on each side. Do not overcook! Sprinkle with salt and pepper. Divide the sauce among four plates. Top with the tuna steaks, and serve.

RED OR WHITE?

Red wine goes with meat and white wine goes with fish is the commonly accepted rule when choosing a wine, and, in general, it's a good one. The higher acidity found in dry white wines adds a pleasant tingle to the flavor of fish and contrasts with its slight sweetness. Simple fish preparations such as broiled or baked fish go well with lighter white wines such as California sauvignon blanc (fumé blanc), Italian Soave or Gavi, and French Muscadet, Pouilly-Fuissé, Pouilly-Fumé, and Chablis. For more complex preparations, such as fish prepared in a cream sauce or with cheese, a richer wine would stand up better. An oaky California Chardonnay would be a good choice.

Of course, there are exceptions to the red wine with fish rule. Fish prepared with tomato sauce, especially one with hearty Mediterranean flavors such as herbs, garlic, and olive oil, is wonderful when served with a robust red wine such as zinfandel or barbera. Salmon, swordfish, and shark steaks have a meaty texture and flavor when grilled and are excellent served with California Merlot or Cabernet Sauvignon.

Whether you play it safe with white or experiment with red, a glass of wine can elevate a fish dinner to new heights.

SAUTEED SOLE with BUTTER-PECAN SAUCE

4–6 servings

Butter-Pecan Sauce

3 tablespoons butter
½ cup chopped pecans
2 tablespoons parsley
1 tablespoon lemon juice
1 teaspoon Worcestershire sauce
½ teaspoon grated lemon peel

½ cup all-purpose flour
1 teaspoon salt
¼ teaspoon cayenne pepper
1½ pounds sole, catfish, or orange roughy
    fillets
3 tablespoons butter
3 tablespoons oil

1. In a small saucepan, melt the butter over low heat. Add the remaining ingredients. Set aside and keep warm.

2. On a piece of wax paper, combine the flour, salt, and pepper. Dip the fillets in flour, and shake to remove excess.

3. In a large skillet over medium high heat, melt the butter with the oil. Add the fish fillets in a single layer. Sauté for 3 to 4 minutes on each side, or until golden brown. With a slotted spatula transfer the fish to a warm platter, spoon on the sauce, and serve.

"Little fish are sweet."

Dutch proverb

STIR-FRIED MONKFISH with PEANUTS

3–4 servings

1 pound monkfish, grouper, or catfish fillets,
     cut into ¾-inch pieces
1 egg white, lightly beaten
1 tablespoon cornstarch
1 tablespoon dry sherry
2 tablespoons soy sauce
1 teaspoon sugar
¼ teaspoon salt
4 tablespoons peanut or vegetable oil
1 teaspoon minced fresh gingerroot
1 garlic clove, minced
1 cup thinly sliced celery
1 cup thinly sliced red pepper
¼ cup chopped scallions
½ cup roasted unsalted peanuts

1. In a bowl combine the fish, egg white, cornstarch, and sherry. Marinate for 30 minutes. In another bowl combine the soy sauce, sugar, and salt.

2. Heat a wok or large skillet over medium-high heat. Add 2 tablespoons oil to the wok and heat until very hot. Add the gingerroot and garlic; stir-fry for 30 seconds. Add the fish and stir-fry another 2 to 3 minutes. Remove with a slotted spoon to a warm platter.

3. Add the remaining oil to the wok. Reduce heat to medium and add the celery, pepper, and scallions. Stir-fry for 3 to 4 minutes.

4. Return the fish to the wok. Add the peanuts and soy sauce mixture. Stir gently until the sauce is thickened.

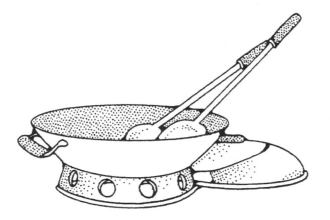

HALIBUT with BLACK BEAN SAUCE

The secret of Chinese cooking is organization. Put the ingredients into small bowls or custard cups and arrange them in order of use next to your stove.

4 servings

1 tablespoon peeled and grated fresh gingerroot
1 teaspoon grated lemon peel
¼ to ½ teaspoon crushed red pepper
3 tablespoons salted fermented black beans
2 teaspoons minced garlic
1 tablespoon dry sherry
1 cup chicken broth
2 tablespoons oyster sauce
1 tablespoon soy sauce
1 teaspoon sugar
⅓ cup plus 1 tablespoon cornstarch
¼ cup water
4 halibut, cod, or tilefish steaks, about ¾
   inch thick
¼ cup peanut oil

1. Combine the gingerroot, lemon peel, and crushed red pepper in a small bowl. In a separate bowl, combine the black beans, garlic, and sherry. In a measuring cup, combine the broth, oyster and soy sauces, and sugar. Blend 1 tablespoon cornstarch with the water.

2. Spread ⅓ cup of cornstarch on a sheet of wax paper. Dip the steaks in cornstarch and shake to remove excess. In a large heavy skillet or wok, heat the oil over medium heat. Add the fish steaks and sauté 3 minutes on each side. Put the fish on a warm serving platter; cover and keep warm.

3. In the same skillet, sauté the ginger mixture for 10 seconds. Add the black bean mixture, and cook for 20 seconds. Add the broth mixture and bring to a boil. Stir the cornstarch and water, and blend into the skillet mixture. Cook, stirring constantly, until thickened. Pour the sauce over steaks and serve immediately.

"Fish, taken collectively in all its species, is to the philosopher an endless source of meditation and surprise."

Brillat-Savarin

SOLE A LA MEUNIERE

This classic French recipe is said to be named for the proverbial miller's wife, who was always lightly coated with flour!

4–6 servings

½ cup flour
½ teaspoon salt
⅛ teaspoon pepper
1½ pounds sole, snapper, or flounder fillets, cut into serving pieces
4 tablespoons clarified butter, or 2 tablespoons butter plus 2 tablespoons vegetable oil
1 tablespoon chopped parsley
2 tablespoons butter
2 tablespoons lemon juice

1. On a sheet of wax paper, combine the flour, salt, and pepper. Dip the fillets into the mixture and shake to remove the excess.

2. Heat a large heavy nonstick skillet over high heat until hot enough to evaporate a drop of water on contact. Add the clarified butter or butter and oil and heat until very hot. Arrange the fillets in the pan in a single layer. Do not crowd the pan. If necessary, sauté the fillets in two batches. Sauté for 1 to 2 minutes on each side, or until golden. With a slotted spatula, transfer fillets to a warm serving platter. Sprinkle with parsley.

3. Wipe out the skillet; place over medium heat. Add the remaining butter and swirl the pan until the butter is melted and golden brown. Remove the pan from the heat; stir in the lemon juice. Spoon over the fish, and serve.

RED SNAPPER PICCATA

4–6 servings

2 eggs
⅓ cup freshly grated Parmesan cheese
¼ cup water
¼ teaspoon salt
⅛ teaspoon pepper
½ cup flour
1½ pounds red snapper, sole, or flounder
　　　fillets, cut into serving pieces
2 tablespoons butter
3 tablespoons olive oil
3 tablespoons fresh lemon juice
2 tablespoons capers, drained and chopped

1. In a bowl, beat together the eggs, cheese, water, salt, and pepper.

2. Spread the flour on a sheet of wax paper. Dip the fillets into the flour and shake to remove the excess.

3. In a large skillet, heat the butter and oil over medium heat. Coat the fillets with the egg mixture. Sauté for 2 to 3 minutes on each side, or until golden. With a slotted spatula, transfer the fillets to a warm serving dish. Cover and keep warm.

4. Add the lemon juice and capers to the skillet. Simmer, stirring constantly, for 1 minute. Pour the sauce over the fillets and serve.

Deep-frying

"With the audacity of true culinary genius,
fried fish is always served cold."

Israel Zangwill

Whether breaded, batter-coated, or simply dusted with seasoned cornmeal, crunchy deep-fried fish is everyone's favorite. For easier handling, cut large fillets or steaks into two or three pieces. Use a deep fryer or deep heavy saucepan with a frying thermometer. Fill the pan no more than half full with fat, but use enough to cover the fish completely.

Crumb coatings will adhere better if the fish is coated and then refrigerated on a rack for 30 minutes to 1 hour before frying. Use tongs to lower the fish gently into the hot fat. A frying basket may be used with breaded fish, but batter-coated fillets will stick to the wire mesh.

The secret of greaseless deep-frying is maintaining an even 375°F. temperature. At that temperature, the coating on the fish will brown evenly and seal in the juices. Most fish will be fried within 3 to 4 minutes. To keep the oil temperature from fluctuating and the pieces from sticking together, fry only a few pieces at a time. Use tongs or a slotted spoon to turn the fish and keep the crust intact. Drain the fish well on a rack or paper towels, and serve immediately. Allow the oil to reach 375°F. again before frying the next batch of fish.

GREEK FRIED COD with SKORDALIA

Skordalia is a creamy garlic sauce that is delicious on fish or steamed vegetables.

4 servings

Skordalia
1 slice firm white bread, crust removed
¼ cup water
3 large garlic cloves
½ teaspoon salt
1 egg yolk
1 tablespoon white wine vinegar
⅛ teaspoon pepper
¾ cup olive oil

1 cup all-purpose flour
¼ teaspoon salt
¼ teaspoon baking powder
⅛ teaspoon pepper
1 to 1¼ cups ice water
Vegetable oil for frying
1 pound cod, pollack, or orange roughy fillets, cut into serving pieces

1. Sprinkle the bread with the water; let stand briefly until softened. Squeeze out the excess moisture.

2. In a blender or food processor, chop the garlic with the salt. Add the softened bread, egg yolk, vinegar, and pepper; blend until smooth. Gradually add the olive oil, a few drops at a time, until the sauce is thickened and smooth. Refrigerate until serving time.

3. In a medium bowl, combine the flour, salt, baking powder, and pepper. Stir in 1 to 1¼ cups ice water to make a batter the thickness of sour cream. The batter should be slightly lumpy.

4. In a deep heavy saucepan or deep fryer, heat the oil to 375°F. Dip the fillets in the batter, and then carefully slip them into the hot oil. Fry the fillets for 3 to 4 minutes, or until golden brown. Drain on paper towels. Serve immediately with the skordalia.

COD

It is estimated that one out of every three fish fillets and steaks eaten in the United States is cut from codfish. Cod has always been an important food source in this country, particularly in New England. In 1784, in recognition of the importance of cod to the economy of the state, a wooden codfish was hung in the Massachusetts House of Representatives. Later, the "Sacred Cod," as it is known, was moved to the House chamber where it still remains, opposite the speaker's desk.

Baby cod weighing less than 3 pounds is often sold as scrod.

CRUNCHY BUTTERMILK FRIED FISH

4 servings

1 pound catfish, flounder, or sole fillets
1 cup buttermilk
1 teaspoon salt
½ teaspoon pepper
¾ cup cornmeal
¼ cup all-purpose flour
Vegetable oil for deep-frying

1. Cut the fillets crosswise into 1-inch strips. In a shallow bowl, combine the buttermilk, salt, and pepper. Add the fish, stirring gently to coat. Cover and refrigerate for 4 hours.

2. In a deep fryer or large heavy saucepan, heat enough oil to 375°F. to cover the fish completely. On a piece of wax paper, combine the cornmeal and flour. Roll the fillets in the cornmeal mixture and shake to remove excess.

3. With tongs, lower the fish into the hot oil. Fry, turning occasionally, until golden brown on all sides, about 3 to 4 minutes. Repeat with the remaining fish. Drain on paper towels and serve immediately.

BEER BATTER FRIED FISH

Serve these fillets English-style, with thick-cut fried potatoes and a sprinkling of malt vinegar.

6 servings

1⅓ cups all-purpose flour
1 teaspoon salt
¼ teaspoon pepper
⅔ cup beer
2 egg yolks, slightly beaten
1 tablespoon melted butter
Vegetable oil for deep-frying
1½ pounds cod, pollack, or whitefish fillets

1. In a medium bowl, combine the flour, salt, and pepper. Stir in the beer, egg yolks, and butter just until the flour is moistened. The batter should be slightly lumpy. Cover and refrigerate for 4 hours or overnight.

2. In a deep heavy saucepan or deep fryer heat enough oil to 375°F. to cover the fillets completely. If large, cut fillets into 4 x 3-inch pieces. Dry them well, then dip into the batter.

3. Carefully lower the fish, a few pieces at a time, into hot oil. Fry for 3 to 4 minutes, or until golden brown on all sides. Repeat with the remaining fish. Drain on paper towels and serve immediately.

FRIED CATFISH with CHUNKY CHILI SAUCE

4–6 servings

Sauce

3 tablespoons vegetable oil
1 green pepper, finely chopped
1 medium onion, finely chopped
1 tablespoon chili powder
1 teaspoon cumin
½ teaspoon oregano
1 can (16 ounces) tomato sauce
½ teaspoon salt
⅛ teaspoon pepper

1½ pounds catfish, sole, or whitefish fillets
½ cup cornmeal
1 teaspoon salt
½ teaspoon cayenne pepper
Oil for deep-frying

1. In a large skillet, heat the oil over medium heat. Add the green pepper and onion and sauté for 5 minutes, or until the onion begins to brown.

2. Stir in the chili powder, cumin, and oregano. Add the tomato sauce, salt, and pepper. Reduce the heat to medium-low, and simmer the sauce for 10 minutes. Set aside.

3. In a deep heavy saucepan or deep fryer, heat the oil to 375°F.

4. Lightly score the skinned sides of the fillets with a sharp knife. On a piece of wax paper, combine the cornmeal, salt, and pepper. Dip the fillets in cornmeal and shake to remove excess. Gently lower the fillets into the hot oil a few pieces at a time. Fry, turning occasionally, until fish is golden, about 3 to 5 minutes. Serve immediately with the sauce.

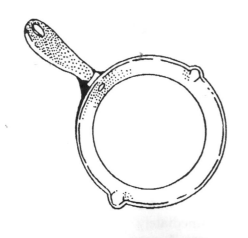

TEMPURA

The secret of a really tender tempura crust is to avoid overblending the batter ingredients. Any type of fish works well in this recipe.

4 servings

Dipping sauce
1 cup beef broth
¼ cup water
¼ cup soy sauce
2 tablespoons dry sherry
1½ teaspoons sugar
1 teaspoon peeled and grated fresh gingerroot
2 tablespoons chopped scallions

Batter
1½ cups cake flour
1½ teaspoons baking powder
¼ teaspoon salt
1¼ cups ice water
1 egg white, lightly beaten

1 pound fish fillets, cut into 3 x 2-inch pieces
4 ounces small mushrooms, trimmed
1 small sweet onion, sliced ¼ inch thick and separated into rings
1 green pepper, seeded and cut into ¼-inch slices
1 medium sweet potato, peeled and cut into ¼-inch slices
Vegetable oil for deep-frying

1. In a medium saucepan, combine all the sauce ingredients. Simmer for 5 minutes. Cool to room temperature.

2. On a piece of wax paper combine the flour, baking powder, and salt. In a medium bowl, blend the water and egg white. Sift the flour mixture into the water and egg white, stirring just until moistened. The batter should be slightly lumpy.

3. In a deep saucepan or deep fryer, heat enough oil to 375°F. to cover the fillets completely. Dip the fish and vegetables a few pieces at a time into the batter. Slip them into hot oil. Fry, turning occasionally, until crisp and lightly browned, about 3 to 4 minutes. Drain on paper towels. Repeat with the remaining fish and vegetables. Serve with dipping sauce.

TOASTED FISH

Similar to shrimp toast, these crispy fish squares make delicious appetizers or can be served as part of a Chinese banquet with stir-fried vegetables.

36 pieces

6 thin slices firm white bread, crusts removed
1 pound sole or flounder fillets
3 eggs
1 teaspoon salt
2 cups fine dry bread crumbs
Peanut or vegetable oil for deep-frying

1. Cut each slice of bread into 6 squares. Cut the fish fillets to fit bread squares.

2. In a shallow dish, beat the eggs with the salt. Spread half the bread crumbs on a sheet of wax paper set on a large cookie sheet. Coat the bread squares with egg, then place them in a single layer on the bread crumbs. Coat the fish squares with egg; top each bread square with a piece of fish. Sprinkle on the remaining bread crumbs. Refrigerate for 30 minutes.

3. Fill a deep fryer or heavy saucepan no more than half full with oil. Heat the oil to 375°F. Place a few pieces of fish in a frying basket and gently lower the fish into the hot oil. Fry for 2 to 3 minutes, turning the fish occasionally until it is crisp and golden brown. Drain on paper towels. Repeat with the remaining fish. Serve with tartar sauce, soy sauce, or hot mustard.

Steaming and Poaching

"Be at ease, I cried with the faith that
moves mountains: the turbot will be cooked
whole, it will be cooked by steam, it is
going to be cooked here and now!"

Brillat-Savarin

Steaming and poaching fish produce the most delicate results of any cooking method. Properly cooked, fillets and steaks will remain moist and tender whether eaten hot or cold.

In steaming, fish are cooked by placing them on a lightly greased metal basket or rack suspended over boiling liquid. The pot is covered and the fish is cooked in the vapors produced by the liquid. Wine, water, clam juice, or milk, either plain or flavored with vegetables and herbs, may be used.

Poaching involves immersing fish in a gently simmering liquid. Fish can be poached on top of the stove, in the oven, or in the microwave (see microwaving section). The important thing to remember is that the liquid must never boil or the fish may break apart. The correct temperature should be very low, with barely a shimmer visible on the surface of the liquid. The poaching liquid can be used to make a sauce or it can be frozen or refrigerated for later use.

CARIBBEAN POACHED RED SNAPPER

4–6 servings

1½ pounds red snapper, perch, or orange
    roughy fillets
1 cup dry white wine
2 tablespoons fresh lemon juice
1 garlic clove, finely chopped
1 small hot chili, seeded and finely chopped
3 cups water
2 carrots, thinly sliced
1 celery stalk, thinly sliced
1 medium onion, thinly sliced
Bouquet garni: 3 sprigs parsley, 2 unpeeled
    garlic cloves, ½ teaspoon whole pepper-
    corns, 1 bay leaf, and ¼ teaspoon dried
    thyme, tied in cheesecloth
½ teaspoon salt
2 tablespoons chopped parsley

1. In a large shallow dish, arrange the fish in a single layer. Add the wine, lemon juice, chopped garlic, and chili. Cover and refrigerate for 1 hour.

2. In a large heavy saucepan, combine the water, carrots, celery, onion, bouquet garni, and salt. Bring to boil over high heat. Reduce heat to medium; cook until the liquid is reduced to 2 cups, about 15 minutes. Remove the bouquet garni.

3. Drain the fish marinade into same saucepan; heat to simmer. Carefully add the fish fillets. Cover and cook for 3 to 5 minutes. With a slotted spatula, transfer the fillets to shallow soup plates. Ladle some of the broth and vegetables over each serving. Sprinkle with chopped parsley. Serve hot or cold.

"The whale that wanders 'round the Pole
Is not a table fish.
You cannot bake or boil him whole
Nor serve him in a dish."
            Hilaire Belloc,
            Bad Child's Book of Beasts

SWORDFISH TONNATO

Vitello tonnato is cold poached veal with a tuna sauce served as an appetizer or main course in Italian restaurants during the summer months. I think it's even better made with fish steaks.

8 servings

Sauce
1 egg
¼ teaspoon salt
1¼ cups mild olive oil
3 tablespoons lemon juice
1 can (7 ounces) tuna in olive oil
5 anchovy fillets, drained
2 tablespoons drained capers

4 cups water
2 cups dry white wine or vermouth
1 small onion, peeled and coarsely chopped
1 celery stalk, coarsely chopped
1 carrot, coarsely chopped
1 bay leaf
Pinch thyme
8 swordfish, tuna, or shark steaks, about
    ½ inch thick
Parsley sprigs, lemon slices, anchovies,
    capers, and black olives, for garnish

1. In a food processor or blender, process the egg and salt until light and frothy. With the machine running, add the olive oil a few drops at a time. Do *not* add the oil quickly or the mixture may curdle.

2. Blend in the lemon juice. Add the canned tuna with oil, anchovies, and capers. Process until smooth. Taste the sauce, adding more lemon juice if desired. Cover and refrigerate.

3. In a large pot, combine the water, wine, onion, celery, carrot, bay leaf, and thyme. Bring to a simmer over medium heat, cover, and cook for 20 minutes.

4. Put the fish steaks in the pot. Add more liquid, if necessary, to just cover the steaks. Return to simmer, cover, and remove from the heat. Let stand for 7 to 8 minutes. With a slotted spatula, remove the steaks from the liquid; pat dry with paper towels.

5. On a large serving platter, spread about one third of the tuna sauce. Arrange the fish steaks on the sauce in a single layer. Spread the remaining sauce on the steaks. Cover and chill for 1 hour.

6. Garnish with parsley sprigs, lemon slices, anchovies, capers, and black olives.

STEAMED FLOUNDER ROLLS

4 servings

2 medium carrots, cut into 3 x ¼-inch strips
2 celery stalks, cut into 3 x ¼-inch strips
4 ounces shiitake, oyster, or white mush-
    rooms, cut into ¼-inch slices
4 tablespoons softened butter
1 scallion, finely chopped
4 flounder or sole fillets, about 1½ pounds
Salt and black pepper to taste
2 tablespoons chopped parsley

1. Bring a medium saucepan of water to a boil. Add the carrots and celery; simmer for 3 minutes. Add the mushrooms and simmer 1 minute more. Drain.

2. In a small bowl, combine 2 tablespoons butter and the scallion. Sprinkle the skinned side of the fillets with salt and pepper. Spread with the butter mixture.

3. Divide the vegetables into four portions. Place one portion at the wide end of each fillet and roll up.

4. In a large saucepan, bring 1 inch of water to the boil. Lightly butter a steamer rack, and place the rolls on the rack. Lower the rack into saucepan. Cover and steam for 4 to 5 minutes. With a slotted spatula, transfer rolls to serving dish.

5. Melt the remaining butter, and spoon over fish. Sprinkle with parsley and serve immediately.

ANCHOVIES

Anchovies always provoke a definite reaction. Because of their strong flavor, people either love them or hate them.

Although fresh anchovies are delicious grilled, most of these tasty little fish are sold preserved. Filleted anchovies can be purchased flat or rolled around capers and canned in olive oil. Those that are packed with capers should be reserved for garnishing.

The best anchovies can be found in Greek, Spanish, or Italian markets. These are layered in salt and sold by weight from a big can. To use them, rinse off the salt under cold running water. Dry the fish with paper towels. Scrape off the skin. With a small knife, separate the anchovy into two fillets and remove the bones. Use immediately or refrigerate covered with olive oil in a closed container for up to 2 weeks.

Anchovy paste is convenient because you don't have to open a whole can for just a few anchovies. The paste comes in a tube like toothpaste and you can squeeze out as much as you need, then recap the tube for later use. It keeps indefinitely. Allow about 1 teaspoon anchovy paste for each anchovy fillet.

Anchovies give a flavor boost to many fish dishes and they have been used as a flavoring ingredient since the time of the ancient Greeks. The Romans, too, appreciated anchovies and made an all-purpose seasoning and sauce called *garum* or *liquamen* from the salted and fermented fish, which was probably the forerunner of today's Worcestershire sauce.

WARM FISH AND PASTA SALAD with ANCHOVY VINAIGRETTE

This combination of hot pasta with fresh vegetables and tender poached fillets is very appealing.

6 servings

Dressing
3 tablespoons lemon juice
3 tablespoons white wine vinegar
1 tablespoon Dijon-style mustard
1 tablespoon anchovy paste or 3 chopped
    anchovies
2 large garlic cloves, minced
½ teaspoon salt
¼ teaspoon freshly ground black pepper
1 cup olive oil

1 pound perch, cod, or snapper fillets
Salt and pepper to taste
1 pound pasta bow ties
2 cups cherry tomatoes, halved
1 small cucumber, seeded and chopped
1 bunch arugula, stems trimmed (about
    3 cups)
1 small red onion, chopped
½ cup chopped fresh basil

1. In a small bowl, whisk together the lemon juice, vinegar, mustard, anchovies, garlic, salt, and pepper. Gradually whisk in the olive oil. Set aside.

2. In a large skillet, bring 1 inch of water to the simmer. Add the fish fillets and salt and pepper to taste. Cover and cook gently for 4 to 5 minutes. Drain the fish and pat dry. Coarsely flake the fish into a bowl. Toss with ½ cup dressing.

3. Cook the pasta until it is firm yet tender to the bite. Drain well; transfer to a large shallow bowl. Toss with the remaining dressing. Stir in the vegetables. Spoon on the fish and sprinkle with the basil. Serve immediately.

"The tide should not go out on a fish before it is in the pan."

Proverb

JAPANESE SEAFOOD HOT POT

If you prefer, you can use two or three varieties of fish instead of the shellfish.

8 servings

1 package (4 ounces) Oriental cellophane noodles
1 bottle (8 ounces) clam juice
1 cup beef broth
1 cup water
⅓ cup soy sauce
⅓ cup dry sherry
2 teaspoons sugar
6 scallions, cut into 1-inch pieces
2 medium carrots, thinly sliced
2 celery stalks, thinly sliced
8 ounces fresh shiitake or button mushrooms, halved or quartered if large
4 ounces fresh spinach, trimmed
1 pound perch, scrod, or snapper fillets, cut into 1-inch pieces
4 ounces small shrimp, shelled and deveined
4 ounces sea scallops, halved or quartered if large

1. Soak the noodles in warm water to cover for 30 minutes. Drain well and cut into 4-inch lengths.

2. In a large saucepan, combine the clam juice, beef broth, water, soy sauce, sherry, and sugar. Bring to a simmer. Add the scallions, carrots, and celery; simmer for 3 minutes. Add the mushrooms and spinach; simmer for 1 minute. Add the fish; simmer for 1 minute. Add the scallops and shrimp; simmer until the shrimp turn pink, about 1 minute. Stir in the noodles. Spoon into heated soup plates and serve.

TIMING

Because fish is naturally tender, it does not need long cooking to soften it. In fact, the longer fish is cooked the more moisture it loses and the tougher it becomes.

As fish cooks, its translucent flesh turns opaque or solid in appearance. When just a thin line of raw translucent flesh remains in the center, the fish is ready to serve. The residual heat will finish the cooking on the way to the table. Fish cooked until it flakes is probably overcooked.

For best texture and flavor, try following the "10-minute rule" developed by the Canadian Department of Fisheries and Oceans. Measure fillets and steaks at the thickest part. Allow 10 minutes cooking time per inch of thickness. For thinner fish, shorten the cooking time proportionately. This method works for broiling, grilling, poaching, and baking. Of course, different factors will affect the cooking time, so use the 10-minute rule just as a guideline. Watch the fish carefully as it cooks and you might find that you prefer fish cooked 7 or 8 minutes to the inch. If fish is cooked in a sauce or wrapped in foil or parchment, add an additional 5 minutes. For frozen fish, double the cooking time to about 20 minutes per inch.

POACHED COD IN CHARDONNAY CREAM

The buttery, vanilla flavors of Chardonnay have a natural affinity for cream and tarragon. Of course, you could substitute another white wine, but Chardonnay would be my first choice.

4 servings

2 cups Chardonnay or other dry white wine
1 cup water
1 onion, chopped
1 carrot, sliced
1 celery stalk, sliced
1 tablespoon chopped parsley
½ teaspoon salt
¼ teaspoon peppercorns
4 cod, tilefish, or salmon steaks, about ¾
    inch thick
1 tablespoon fresh tarragon, or 1 teaspoon
    dried
½ cup heavy cream

1. In a large skillet, combine the Chardonnay, water, onion, carrot, celery, parsley, salt, and peppercorns. Bring to a simmer over medium heat. Arrange the fish steaks in the skillet in a single layer. Reduce heat to low. Cover and simmer for 8 to 10 minutes. With a slotted spatula, carefully remove the fish steaks to a warm serving platter. Cover and keep warm.

2. Strain the poaching liquid. Return 1 cup liquid to the skillet; add the tarragon. Boil rapidly over high heat until the liquid is reduced by half. Add the cream and simmer for 1 minute. Spoon over fish and serve.

HELEN'S SEVICHE

This recipe was suggested by Helen Siller, who specializes in fish cookery. The acid in the lime juice "cooks" these fillets to a tender consistency similar to that of poached fish. It's a perfect luncheon dish or appetizer for a hot summer day.

4 servings

1 pound skinless snapper, scrod, or halibut fillets, cut into 1-inch pieces
1 cup freshly squeezed lime juice
2 medium ripe tomatoes, seeded and chopped
1 ripe avocado, peeled and cut into ½-inch dice
¼ cup finely chopped scallion

¼ cup chopped fresh coriander
2 to 4 tablespoons hot chilies, seeded and finely chopped
1 teaspoon salt
⅛ teaspoon freshly ground pepper
¼ cup light olive oil

1. In a small deep bowl, combine the fish and lime juice. Cover and refrigerate 4 hours, or until fish is no longer translucent, stirring occasionally.

2. Drain the fish, reserving lime juice. Transfer the fish to a large serving platter.

3. Combine the tomatoes, avocado, scallion, coriander, chilies, salt, pepper, and olive oil. Spoon over the fish and stir gently. Taste for seasoning, adding lime juice as needed.

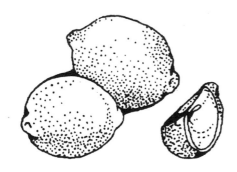

Baking

"Fish Baked in Ashes: No cheese, no nonsense! Just place it tenderly in fig leaves and tie them on top with a string; then push it under hot ashes, bethinking thee wisely of the time when it is done, and burn it not up."

Archestratus
Gastrology, 4 B.C.

Baking is one of the easiest ways to prepare fish steaks and fillets but because of the dry heat involved in the cooking, care must be taken to prevent the fish from drying out. For that reason, fish is usually baked with a sauce or liquid, such as wine or chicken or fish stock, basted with butter or oil, or wrapped in leaves, foil, or parchment paper. Fatty fish such as salmon, bluefish, and mackerel fare especially well when baked.

DONNA'S HERBED SOLE EN PAPILLOTE

The culinary term *en papillote* is French for fish or other foods baked in a paper package, usually parchment or foil. The name is derived from *papillon,* meaning butterfly, the classic shape of the paper before folding. As the fish bakes, its flavors mingle with the savory herbs and vegetables in the package. Steam is created so that the package emerges from the oven dramatically puffed. Each diner tears open his own package, revealing the contents and releasing the aromatic steam.

This recipe was given to me by Donna Boland, a good friend and an excellent cook. It's just right for an intimate dinner for two, served with a rice pilaf and a bottle of lightly chilled Chablis.

2 servings

3 tablespoons melted butter
10 sprigs watercress, tough stems removed
2 sole, flounder, or whitefish fillets
2 tablespoons minced shallots
2 medium mushrooms, trimmed and thinly
    sliced
2 tablespoons julienned carrot
¼ cup seeded and chopped tomato

2 sprigs fresh thyme, or a pinch dried
2 tablespoons dry white wine or vermouth
Salt and pepper to taste

1. Preheat the oven to 400°F. Fold 2 15 x 20-inch sheets of parchment paper or aluminum foil in half crosswise to make 15 x 10-inch rectangles. Cut each into a heart shape about 14 inches long by 8 inches wide.

2. Open each heart and brush with ½ tablespoon butter. Place 5 sprigs of watercress in the center of half of each heart. Place a fillet on top of the watercress. Brush the fillets with butter.

3. Scatter the shallots, mushrooms, and carrot over the fillets. Sprinkle with tomato, thyme, wine, remaining butter, and salt and pepper to taste.

4. Fold the other half of the heart over the fish. Starting at the rounded top, seal the edges by making a series of tight overlapping folds. Place on a cookie sheet, and bake for 8 minutes. Serve immediately.

"Fish must swim thrice—once in water, a second time in the sauce, and a third time in wine in the stomach."
John Ray, 1627–1705

HALIBUT STEAKS IN GREEN SAUCE

In Spain, this dish is baked and served in individual earthenware casseroles, accompanied by boiled potatoes or chunks of hot, crusty bread.

4 servings

12 small clams or mussels
½ cup plus 2 tablespoons flour
1 teaspoon salt
¼ teaspoon pepper
4 halibut, cod, or tilefish steaks
¼ cup plus 2 tablespoons olive oil
4 garlic cloves, finely chopped
⅓ cup finely chopped scallions
1 bottle (8 ounces) clam juice
¾ cup dry white wine
½ cup finely chopped parsley
1 cup fresh or frozen thawed peas
Salt and pepper to taste

1. Soak the clams or mussels in cold, salted water for 30 minutes to 1 hour, changing the water two or three times. Scrub the shells thoroughly under cold running water. If using mussels, pull off the beards with a small knife.

2. Preheat the oven to 350°F. On a piece of wax paper combine ½ cup flour, salt, and pepper. Dip the fish in the flour mixture, and shake to remove the excess.

3. Heat a large skillet over medium-high heat until it is hot enough to evaporate a drop of water on contact. Add ¼ cup oil and heat until the oil is very hot. Add the steaks and sauté until lightly browned, about 2 minutes on each side. Transfer the steaks to an 8 x 12-inch baking dish. Wipe out the skillet.

4. In the same skillet, heat the remaining oil over medium heat. Add the garlic and scallions, and sauté for 2 to 3 minutes, until the garlic is golden. Stir in 2 tablespoons flour; cook 30 seconds. Gradually blend in the clam juice and wine. Bring to a simmer, and cook until slightly thickened, about 2 minutes. Stir in parsley, peas, and salt and pepper to taste.

5. Spoon the sauce over fish. Arrange clams or mussels around steaks. Bake 20 minutes. Discard any clams or mussels that have not opened.

LOUISE'S MACKEREL OREGANATA

The bread crumb topping in this recipe is my mom's favorite all-purpose fish seasoning. Despite the name, she never uses oregano because she doesn't like the flavor! I think it's delicious with or without. Try it as a topping for baked clams or mussels, too.

4–6 servings

1 ½ pounds mackerel, bluefish, or cod fillets in serving pieces
½ cup fine, dry bread crumbs, preferably from Italian or French bread
¼ cup freshly grated Parmesan or Romano cheese

¼ cup finely chopped parsley
2 to 3 tablespoons olive oil
½ teaspoon oregano (optional)
¼ teaspoon salt
⅛ teaspoon pepper
Lemon wedges

1. Preheat the oven to 450°F. Lightly oil a baking dish large enough to hold the fish in a single layer. Arrange the fillets in the dish skin-side down.

2. In a bowl, combine the bread crumbs, cheese, parsley, 2 tablespoons olive oil, oregano, salt, and pepper. Spoon over the fillets. If using lean fillets such as cod, drizzle with an additional tablespoon of olive oil.

3. Bake for 5 to 8 minutes. Serve immediately with lemon wedges.

SALMON with CHIVE BEURRE BLANC

These colorful salmon packages are elegant enough for a dinner party.

4 servings

¼ cup minced shallots
1 tablespoon butter
16 large spinach leaves (about 8 ounces), stems removed
1 ½ pounds skinless salmon fillet, cut into 4 pieces
1 tablespoon chopped fresh tarragon, or ½ teaspoon dried
Salt
Freshly ground white pepper
¼ cup melted butter
⅓ cup dry white wine
2 tablespoons fresh lemon juice
1 cup (2 sticks) chilled butter, cut into ½-inch pieces
2 tablespoons minced fresh chives
Whole chives for garnish

1. Preheat the oven to 375°F. Butter a 9-inch square baking dish.

2. In a small skillet, sauté the shallots in butter over medium-low heat until tender, about 3 to 4 minutes.

3. Bring a large pot of water to the boil. Blanch the spinach for 30 seconds, or until just wilted. Immediately place the leaves in ice water to stop the cooking. Drain and pat dry with paper towels.

4. Sprinkle the salmon with tarragon, salt, and pepper. Spread 1 tablespoon sautéed shallots on each piece. Drizzle with half of the melted butter.

5. On a flat surface, overlap 4 spinach leaves. Roll up 1 piece of salmon and place on top of the spinach. Fold the spinach over salmon to enclose completely. Repeat with the remaining salmon and spinach leaves. Place each package seam-side down in the prepared baking dish. Brush with the remaining butter, and cover tightly with foil. Bake for 20 to 25 minutes.

6. In a small saucepan, combine the wine and lemon juice. Simmer over medium heat until it is reduced to 1 tablespoon, and reduce heat to low. With a whisk, beat in the chilled butter one piece at a time. Do not allow the sauce to boil. Stir in the chives and additional salt and pepper to taste. Spoon some of the sauce onto 4 plates. Top with salmon packages and spoon on remaining sauce. Garnish with whole chives, if desired.

"These shall ye eat of all that are in the waters: whatsoever hath fins and scales in the waters, in the seas, and in the rivers, them shall ye eat."

Leviticus XI

ORANGE SOLE ROLL-UPS

2 servings

2 tablespoons butter
¼ cup finely chopped shallots
1 teaspoon grated orange peel
Pinch dried thyme
2 sole or flounder fillets, about 6 ounces each
Salt
Freshly ground pepper
¼ cup orange juice
¼ cup dry white wine or vermouth
1 teaspoon cornstarch blended with 1 table-
　　spoon water

1. Preheat the oven to 375°F. Butter an 8-inch square baking dish.

2. In a small skillet, melt the butter over medium heat and sauté the shallots until tender. Remove from heat. Stir in the orange peel and thyme.

3. Cut the fillets in half lengthwise. Sprinkle the skinned side with salt and pepper. Spread with half the shallot mixture. Starting at the wide end, roll up each piece. Stand rolls on end in the prepared baking dish. Add the orange juice and white wine. Drizzle with the remaining shallot butter. Bake for 20 to 25 minutes, or until fish is just opaque in center.

4. Drain the cooking liquid into a small saucepan. Cover rolls and keep them warm. Bring the liquid to a simmer. Stir in the cornstarch mixture; simmer for 1 minute more. Spoon over the fillets and serve immediately.

PAUPIETTES, ROLL-UPS, AND TURBANS

Paupiettes, roll-ups, and turbans are three names for the same type of preparation. To prepare, choose fillets that are ¼ to ½ inch thick. If the fillets are wider than 2½ inches at their widest point, cut them in half lengthwise. Stuff or season the fish as indicated in the recipe, then roll up fillets from the wider end. Carefully stand the rolled-up fillets on the cut or flatter end.

CHEESE-FILLED FISH ROULADES

4 servings

2 large or 4 small flounder, sole, or whitefish
    fillets
Salt and pepper to taste
1 cup (about 4 ounces) grated muenster or
    Monterey Jack cheese
2 tablespoons chopped parsley
2 tablespoons mayonnaise
1 tablespoon grated onion
1 teaspoon thyme
½ teaspoon paprika

1. Preheat the oven to 400°F. Butter a 9-inch square baking pan.

2. Cut large fillets in half lengthwise. Sprinkle skinned side with salt and pepper.

3. In a small bowl, combine cheese, parsley, mayonnaise, onion, thyme, and paprika. Spread mixture over fillets. Roll up from wide end. Place rolls flat or cut-side down in prepared pan. Bake 15 minutes. Transfer to broiler. Broil 3 minutes, or until lightly browned.

FLOUNDER STUFFED with CRAB

Many fish markets feature prepared crab-stuffed fillets, but they're even better when homemade.

6 servings

2 tablespoons butter
¼ cup finely chopped onion
¼ cup finely chopped celery
8 ounces crabmeat, picked over
¼ cup mayonnaise
2 tablespoons Dijon-style mustard
1 tablespoon lemon juice
Dash hot pepper sauce
Paprika
6 flounder or sole fillets
Salt and pepper to taste
2 tablespoons melted butter

1. Preheat the oven to 400°F. Butter a 9-inch square baking dish. In a small skillet, melt butter over medium heat. Add onion and celery, and sauté until tender, about 5 minutes.

2. In a medium bowl, combine crabmeat, mayonnaise, mustard, lemon juice, hot pepper sauce, and a pinch of paprika. Blend in onion and celery.

3. Sprinkle skinned side of fillets with salt and pepper to taste. Divide crab mixture into six portions and place one portion at the wide end of each fillet. Roll up fillets and place seam-side down in prepared baking dish. Brush with melted butter and sprinkle with paprika. Bake 20 minutes.

RED SNAPPER with 30 CLOVES OF GARLIC

This recipe was inspired by the roast chicken with 40 cloves of garlic made famous by the late James Beard. The slowly cooked garlic cloves have a mild, nutty flavor that's delicious with fish fillets.

6–8 servings

2 whole heads of garlic, peeled (about
    30 cloves)
Olive oil
¼ teaspoon dried marjoram
Salt and pepper to taste
2 pounds red snapper, sole, or flounder fillets
1½ teaspoons fresh thyme, or ½ teaspoon
    dried
¼ cup dry white wine
2 tablespoons lemon juice

1. In a small skillet, combine garlic cloves with enough oil to barely cover them. Sprinkle with marjoram and salt and pepper to taste. Cook over very low heat, stirring occasionally until the garlic is tender and golden, about 10 minutes.

2. Preheat the oven to 400°F. Lightly brush a baking dish just large enough to hold fillets in a single layer with some of the garlic oil. Add the fillets and sprinkle with additional salt and pepper and thyme. With a slotted spoon, remove the garlic cloves from saucepan and scatter them over the fillets. Pour the wine and lemon juice over fillets and drizzle with 3 tablespoons of garlic oil. Bake for 5 to 8 minutes and serve immediately.

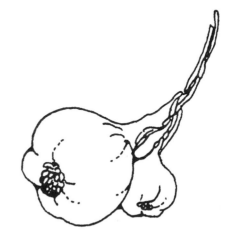

BLUEFISH with ROSEMARY POTATOES

Crispy potato slices are a nice contrast to the tender fish fillets.

8 servings

1 ½ pounds all-purpose potatoes, peeled and
    thinly sliced
⅓ cup olive oil
3 large garlic cloves, minced
1 ½ teaspoons dried rosemary, crumbled
½ teaspoon salt
¼ teaspoon black pepper
2 pounds bluefish, mackerel, or mullet fillets
3 tablespoons fresh lemon juice
2 tablespoons chopped fresh parsley

1. Preheat the oven to 450°F. Oil a 10 x 15-inch jelly roll pan.

2. Combine the potatoes with half the olive oil, garlic, rosemary, salt, and pepper. Spread the potatoes evenly in the pan. Bake for 20 minutes, or until the potatoes begin to brown.

3. Remove the pan from the oven. With a metal spatula, turn the potatoes over. Bake for 10 minutes. Arrange the fish on top of the potatoes. Sprinkle with the remaining ingredients and bake for 15 minutes. Serve immediately.

BLUEFISH with CRUMB TOPPING

4–6 servings

1 ½ pounds bluefish, pollack, or orange
    roughy fillets
Salt and pepper to taste
2 tablespoons olive oil
1 can (2 ounces) anchovy fillets, drained
1 teaspoon dried rosemary, crumbled
½ cup fine dry bread crumbs
2 tablespoons chopped parsley

1. Preheat the oven to 400°F. Oil a baking pan large enough to hold the fish in a single layer.

2. Sprinkle the fillets with salt and pepper to taste. Place them in the prepared baking dish.

3. In a small saucepan, heat the olive oil over medium heat. Stir in the anchovies and rosemary. Cook for 2 minutes, or until the anchovies are dissolved. Remove from heat. Stir in the bread crumbs and parsley.

4. Spread the bread crumb mixture over fish. Bake for 5 to 8 minutes.

BAKED MONKFISH with RATATOUILLE

Ratatouille is a savory vegetable stew that is delicious by itself or baked with fish. You can make it ahead of time and refrigerate it, but reheat gently before adding fish.

6 servings

1 medium eggplant (about 1 pound), cut into
    ¾-inch cubes
2 teaspoons salt
7 tablespoons olive oil
8 ounces mushrooms, halved or quartered if
    large
1 large red or green pepper, cut into ¾-inch
    pieces
1 large onion, thinly sliced
3 teaspoons minced garlic
1 teaspoon dried marjoram
½ teaspoon dried thyme
⅛ teaspoon freshly ground pepper
1 large tomato, seeded and chopped
2 tablespoons chopped fresh parsley
1½ pounds monkfish, cod, or grouper fillets

1. Place the eggplant in a colander set over a large bowl; toss with salt and allow to drain for 1 hour. Pat dry with paper towels.

2. In a large heavy skillet, heat 2 tablespoons oil over high heat. Add the mushrooms, pepper, and onion. Sauté for 5 minutes or until the vegetables begin to brown. Remove the vegetables to a bowl.

3. In the same skillet, heat 4 tablespoons oil. Add the eggplant and 2 teaspoons garlic, and sauté for 4 minutes. Return the vegetables to the pan. Stir in the marjoram, thyme, and pepper; cover, and simmer over medium heat for 3 minutes, or until the vegetables are tender. Add the tomato and parsley; sauté over high heat for 1 minute. Spoon the ratatouille into an 8 x 12-inch baking dish.

4. Preheat the oven to 375°F. Sprinkle the fish with salt and pepper and rub it with remaining 1 teaspoon garlic and 1 tablespoon oil. Place the fish on top of ratatouille, spooning some of the vegetables over the fish. Bake for 30 minutes, or until the fish is cooked through and the ratatouille is bubbling.

TROUT with SHIITAKE AND BACON

Shiitake are cultivated Japanese mushrooms with a delicious woodsy flavor. If they are unavailable, substitute white mushrooms or another wild mushroom.

4 servings

8 ounces shiitake or white mushrooms
5 slices (4 ounces) bacon
1 garlic clove, minced
¼ cup beef broth
Salt and pepper to taste
4 trout or pike fillets
1 tablespoon lemon juice
2 tablespoons chopped fresh parsley

1. Preheat oven to 425°F. Remove tough stems from shiitake mushrooms or trim white mushrooms. Halve or quarter mushrooms if large. Lightly oil a baking dish large enough to hold fillets in a single layer.

2. In a large skillet, fry bacon over medium heat until almost crisp, about 5 minutes. With a slotted spoon, remove the bacon and reserve the drippings in the skillet. Add mushrooms, garlic, and broth. Sprinkle with salt and pepper to taste. Cook 8 minutes, or until mushrooms are tender and most of the liquid evaporates. Coarsely chop bacon.

3. Arrange trout skin-side down in the prepared baking dish; sprinkle with salt, pepper, and lemon juice. Spoon mushrooms over fish. Top with bacon and parsley. Bake 10 minutes.

BAKED COD IN TOMATO AND SHALLOT SAUCE

4–6 servings

Sauce

2 tablespoons olive oil
¼ cup finely chopped shallots
1 can (16 ounces) Italian peeled tomatoes, chopped
½ cup dry white wine
½ teaspoon rosemary
½ teaspoon salt
⅛ teaspoon pepper

1½ pounds cod, pollack, or orange roughy fillets
½ cup fresh bread crumbs
¼ cup chopped fresh parsley
1 tablespoon olive oil

1. In a large saucepan, heat the olive oil over medium heat. Sauté the shallots for 5 minutes, or until softened. Add the remaining sauce ingredients. Simmer for 30 minutes, stirring occasionally, until thick.

2. Preheat the oven to 400°F. Oil a baking dish large enough to hold the fillets in a single layer. Place the fillets in the dish and sprinkle with salt and pepper. Spoon the sauce over the fish. Bake for 5 minutes. Combine the bread crumbs and parsley, and sprinkle over the fish. Drizzle with the oil. Bake for 5 to 8 minutes. Transfer to the broiler; broil 1 to 2 minutes, until crumbs are brown.

SEA TROUT with CHILIES AND SOUR CREAM

4–6 servings

1½ pounds sea trout, salmon, or sea bass
    fillets
Salt and pepper to taste
1 tablespoon fresh lemon or lime juice
1 tablespoon softened butter
¼ cup sour cream
1 tablespoon chopped chives
1 to 2 teaspoons minced fresh chilies

1. Preheat the oven to 400°F. Butter a baking dish large enough to hold the fillets in a single layer. Arrange the fish in the dish.

2. Sprinkle the fillets with salt, pepper, and lemon juice. Spread with the butter.

3. Combine the sour cream, chives, and chilies; spoon over the fillets. Bake for 6 to 8 minutes.

BAKED HALIBUT with ESCARGOT BUTTER

The garlicky butter topping is the best reason I can think of for eating baked snails! It's just as delicious baked on halibut or other fish steaks. Leftovers can be frozen or tossed with vegetables or noodles. Other flavored butters can be found starting on page 89.

4 servings

½ cup butter, softened
2 tablespoons finely chopped scallions
1 large garlic clove, minced
2 tablespoons chopped parsley

Salt and pepper to taste
4 halibut, cod, or tilefish steaks, about
    ¾ inch thick

1. Preheat the oven to 400°F. Butter a baking dish large enough to hold the fish in one layer.

2. In a small bowl, combine the butter, scallions, garlic, parsley, and salt and pepper to taste.

3. Arrange the fish in the prepared baking dish and sprinkle with salt and pepper. Bake for 5 minutes. Top each steak with 1 to 2 tablespoons of prepared butter. Bake for an additional 1 to 2 minutes.

Microwaving

"Fish dinners will make a man spring like a flea."

**Thomas Jordan,
1612–1685**

Microwaving is ideal for cooking fish fillets and fish steaks. It is superquick and easy, and there is little cleanup afterward. Microwaved fish are very moist and tender. Since cooking time is so brief, special care should be taken not to overcook the fish.

Choose a flat, shallow microwave-safe dish. Arrange fish with thicker portions toward the outside of the dish. Very thin fillets can be overlapped or folded to make the cooking more uniform.

Cover dish with plastic wrap, turning back one corner of the plastic to allow steam to escape. All microwave ovens differ, but in general, 3 minutes per pound of boneless fish at high power is about right. If your microwave oven is not equipped with a carousel, rotate the dish halfway through the cooking time. Thinner fillets and steaks should be served immediately, while thicker fish should be allowed to stand briefly so that heat can penetrate the center of the fish and finish the cooking.

SALMON with CAVIAR SAUCE

Use whatever kind of caviar you like. Coral-colored salmon caviar is especially pretty, as is golden white-fish caviar. Garnish plates with watercress, lettuce, and hard-boiled eggs for a complete meal.

6 servings

½ cup chopped carrot
½ cup chopped celery
½ cup chopped onion
2 whole cloves
1 bay leaf
½ teaspoon salt
2 cups water
1 cup dry white wine or vermouth
2 tablespoons fresh lemon juice
6 salmon, halibut, or tilefish steaks, about
    ¾ inch thick

Caviar Sauce
8 ounces sour cream
3 ounces caviar, preferably salmon or white-fish
2 tablespoons chopped scallions

1. In a large microwave-safe covered casserole or bowl, combine the carrot, celery, onion, cloves, bay leaf, salt, water, wine, and lemon juice. Cover and microwave on high until the mixture comes to a boil, about 8 to 10 minutes.

2. Add the salmon and cover. Microwave on high for 3 minutes, then let fish stand for 5 minutes. Chill until serving time.

3. Just before serving, gently stir together the sour cream, 2 ounces of caviar, and scallions.

4. Remove the salmon steaks from the liquid with a slotted spatula. Pat them dry with paper towels. Scrape off the skin.

5. Arrange the fish on serving plates. Spoon on the caviar sauce and garnish with the remaining caviar.

TILEFISH with CITRUS AND CHIVES

The clean, sunny flavors of citrus peel are a wonderful combination with fish. When grating, turn the fruit often to avoid digging into the bitter white pith.

2 servings

2 tilefish, halibut, or cod steaks, about
    ¾ inch thick
Salt and pepper
2 tablespoons softened butter
¼ teaspoon grated lemon peel
¼ teaspoon grated orange peel
¼ teaspoon grated lime peel
1 tablespoon chopped chives

1. Place the fish steaks in a 9-inch square microwave-safe baking dish. Sprinkle with salt and pepper.

2. In a small bowl, blend the remaining ingredients. Spread over the fish. Cover with plastic wrap, turning up one corner to vent.

3. Microwave on high for 3 minutes. Let stand 5 minutes before serving.

"Nonsense and alas! How can I possibly be sure that anyone could survive, in a country where there is no fresh sea fish?"
Brillat-Savarin

FISH FILLETS SCAMPI-STYLE

3–4 servings

2 tablespoons olive oil
2 tablespoons butter
2 garlic cloves, finely chopped
1 medium ripe tomato, seeded and finely
    chopped
2 tablespoons chopped parsley
2 tablespoons lemon juice
½ teaspoon oregano
½ teaspoon salt
¼ teaspoon pepper
1 pound fish fillets, cut into 4 pieces

1. In an 8 x 12-inch microwave-safe baking dish, combine oil, butter, and garlic. Cover with plastic wrap, turning up one corner to vent, and microwave on high for 1 ½ minutes. Scrape into a small bowl. Stir in tomato, parsley, lemon juice, oregano, salt, and pepper.

2. Arrange fillets in a single layer in the baking dish. Spoon tomato mixture over fish. Cover with plastic wrap, turning up one corner to vent. Microwave on high for 3 minutes. Serve immediately.

CHILLED SOLE with CORIANDER

These fillets are great for a picnic or outdoor party. Serve with plenty of pita bread to mop up the delicious marinade.

4–6 servings

Marinade
½ cup olive oil
3 tablespoons white wine vinegar
½ cup chopped fresh coriander
⅓ cup finely chopped red onion
1 teaspoon paprika
1 teaspoon grated lemon peel
1 teaspoon ground coriander
1 teaspoon salt

½ teaspoon ground cumin
Pinch cayenne pepper

1½ pounds sole, cod, or snapper fillets
Whole coriander leaves

1. In a medium bowl, whisk together marinade ingredients.

2. Place fillets in a single layer in a microwave-safe baking dish. Top each fillet with four or five coriander leaves. Cover with plastic wrap, turning up one corner to vent. Microwave on high for 4 minutes.

3. Uncover fillets and pour on marinade. Cover and chill until serving time.

LEMON-SESAME FLOUNDER

3–4 servings

3 tablespoons butter
2 tablespoons chopped scallions
3 tablespoons lemon juice
½ teaspoon grated lemon peel
1 pound flounder, sole, or snapper fillets
2 tablespoons toasted sesame seeds
Salt and pepper to taste

1. In a microwave-safe 8 x 12-inch dish, combine butter and scallions. Cover with plastic wrap, turning up one end to vent. Cook on high for 1½ minutes.

2. Uncover, and stir in lemon juice and peel. Dip fish fillets in mixture to coat both sides. Arrange fillets skinned-side down in a single layer. Sprinkle with sesame seeds, and salt and pepper to taste. Cover with plastic wrap, turning up one end to vent. Microwave on high for 3 minutes. Serve immediately.

STRIPED BASS with FENNEL

The sweet, subtle taste of fennel, sometimes called anise, is wonderful with mild fish fillets.

3–4 servings

1 large fennel bulb, about 1 pound
3 tablespoons butter
1 medium onion, chopped
½ teaspoon grated orange peel
1 pound striped bass, snapper, or sole fillets
2 teaspoons fresh lemon juice
Salt and pepper to taste

1. Cut fennel in half lengthwise; discard tough stems. Cut into very thin crosswise slices.

2. Place butter in an 8 x 12-inch microwave-safe dish. Cover with plastic wrap, turning up one corner to vent. Microwave on high for 30 seconds. Stir in fennel, onion, and orange peel. Cover, and microwave on high for 6 minutes. Let stand for 3 minutes.

3. Arrange fillets over fennel in dish. Sprinkle with lemon juice and salt and pepper to taste. Spoon some of the fennel over the fillets, cover, and microwave on high for 3 minutes. Serve immediately.

SOLE with VERMOUTH AND VEGETABLES

Although the manufacturers keep their exact formulas closely guarded secrets, dry white vermouth is made from a base of white wine flavored with orange peel, cloves, cinnamon, and other fruits, herbs, and spices. It is handy for cooking purposes because, unlike wine, it keeps indefinitely. Keep some on hand so you won't have to open a whole bottle of wine for recipes like this one, which calls for just a small amount.

3–4 servings

1 red pepper, seeded and thinly sliced
2 scallions, julienned
4 ounces mushrooms, trimmed and thinly
    sliced
Salt and pepper to taste
2 tablespoons white vermouth or dry white
    wine
1 pound sole, orange roughy, or scrod fillets
¼ cup chopped fresh dill
1 tablespoon butter

1. In an 8 x 12-inch microwave-safe dish, combine the red pepper, scallions, and mushrooms. Sprinkle with salt and pepper to taste and 1 tablespoon vermouth. Cover with plastic wrap, turning up one corner to vent. Microwave on high for 4 minutes.

2. Arrange fillets over vegetables. Sprinkle fish with remaining vermouth, salt and pepper to taste, and dill. Dot with butter. Cover with plastic wrap, turning up one corner. Microwave on high for 3 minutes. Serve immediately.

ORIENTAL FLOUNDER

3–4 servings

1 pound flounder, sole, or whitefish fillets
½ cup thinly sliced scallions
3 tablespoons soy sauce
2 tablespoons rice wine vinegar
1 tablespoon Oriental sesame oil
1 teaspoon grated peeled fresh gingerroot
½ teaspoon grated orange peel
Pinch cayenne pepper

1. Arrange the fish fillets in a single layer in a microwave-safe dish. Sprinkle with the scallions. Combine the remaining ingredients and pour over fish. Cover with plastic wrap, turning up one corner to vent.

2. Microwave on high for 3 minutes. Serve immediately.

TILEFISH with SPINACH AND OREGANO

2 servings

2 tablespoons olive oil
1 garlic clove, minced
10 ounces spinach, stems removed
1 teaspoon oregano
Salt and pepper to taste
2 tilefish, cod, or swordfish steaks, about
    ¾ inch thick
2 teaspoons lemon juice

1. In a 9-inch square microwave-safe dish, combine the olive oil and garlic. Cover with plastic wrap, turning up one corner to vent, and microwave on high for 1½ minutes.

2. Arrange the spinach in dish, tossing to coat with oil. Sprinkle with ½ teaspoon oregano and salt and pepper to taste. Cover with plastic wrap, turning up one corner, and microwave on high for 2 minutes.

3. Arrange the fish steaks over the spinach, and sprinkle with lemon juice, remaining oregano, and additional salt and pepper to taste. Cover with plastic wrap, turning up one corner, and microwave on high for 3 minutes. Let stand, covered, 3 minutes before serving.

> **"What an idiot is man to believe that abstaining from flesh, and eating fish, which is so much more delicate and delicious, constitutes fasting."**
> **Napoleon I, 1769–1821**

Braising and Stewing

> "Stepping to the kitchen door, I uttered the word 'cod' with great emphasis, and resumed my seat. In a few moments the savory steam came forth again, but with a different flavor, and in good time a fine cod-chowder was placed before us."
> **Herman Melville, *Moby Dick***

Braising and stewing are techniques similar to poaching. Braised fish fillets or steaks also are cooked in a sauce, but here much less liquid is used and the sauce is denser and more concentrated.

When stewed, the fish steaks or fillets are gently simmered in a large quantity of a liquid, usually in the form of a sauce that has been flavored with herbs and aromatic vegetables.

Firm-fleshed fish such as cod, monkfish, grouper, tilefish, and catfish generally fare better when braised or stewed because they are less likely to fall apart in cooking. No matter what kind of fish you choose, be sure to keep cooking time to the minimum. Stews and braises can be prepared in advance and, in fact, often taste better if they are, so they are perfect for entertaining. But add the fish just before you are ready to serve for the best results.

Also included in this chapter are several recipes for pasta sauces and chowders, which are variations on the braising and stewing techniques.

BRAISED SOLE with TOMATOES AND MUSHROOMS

This easy and elegant dish goes well with buttered egg noodles.

4–6 servings

4 tablespoons·butter
2 tablespoons finely chopped shallots or
    onions
1 cup thinly sliced mushrooms
1½ pounds sole, catfish, or whitefish fillets
Salt and pepper to taste
½ cup dry white wine
1 medium tomato, seeded and chopped
    (about ½ cup)
2 tablespoons finely chopped parsley

1. In a large skillet, melt 3 tablespoons butter over medium heat. Add the shallots or onion, and sauté for 5 minutes, until tender. Add the mushrooms, and sauté until they begin to brown, about 5 minutes.

2. Sprinkle sole with salt and pepper to taste. Place in pan in a single layer over the mushrooms and shallots. Add the wine, tomato, and parsley, and bring to a simmer. Reduce heat to low, cover, and cook for 2 minutes, until fish is just cooked.

3. With a slotted spatula, remove the fillets to serving plates. Raise heat and stir until the sauce is reduced and thickened. Adjust seasoning. Remove the sauce from the heat and swirl in remaining tablespoon of butter. Spoon over fillets, and serve immediately.

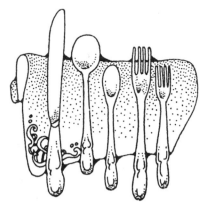

ZUPPA DI PESCE with GARLIC CROUTONS

This savory Italian fish stew is even more interesting when made with more than one variety of fish. Or stir in a dozen scrubbed mussels or small clams when adding the fish.

6–8 servings

1 loaf French bread
Whole peeled garlic cloves
½ cup olive oil
½ cup chopped onion
3 large garlic cloves, finely chopped
¼ cup chopped fresh parsley
¾ cup dry white wine
1 can (28 ounces) Italian peeled tomatoes, chopped
1 teaspoon oregano
1 teaspoon salt
¼ teaspoon pepper
2 pounds ocean perch, rockfish, or sea bass, cut into 2-inch chunks

1. Preheat oven to 400°F. Slice bread into ½-inch diagonal slices. Place on a cookie sheet and bake 10 minutes, or until browned. Rub each slice with garlic; set aside.

2. In a large Dutch oven, heat the olive oil over medium heat. Add the onion and sauté until tender, about 5 minutes. Add the chopped garlic and 2 tablespoons of parsley, and sauté for 30 seconds. Add wine and simmer 1 minute. Stir in the tomatoes with their juice, oregano, salt, and pepper. Cook for 10 minutes.

3. Gently add the fish, cover, and cook for 5 minutes. Place 2 or 3 croutons in each soup plate. Spoon fish over croutons; sprinkle with remaining parsley.

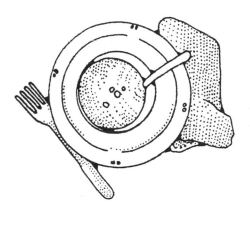

CORN AND FISH CHOWDER

Chowders and stews are good ways to use frozen fish fillets, since the fish does not need to be thawed before cooking. Just adjust the cooking time accordingly.

4–6 servings

4 tablespoons butter
2 carrots, peeled and thinly sliced
1 large onion, chopped
½ cup thinly sliced celery
1 bottle (8 ounces) clam juice
~~1 cup~~ water *(¼ c. water)*
½ teaspoon salt
⅛ teaspoon cayenne pepper

Pinch nutmeg
1 pound cod or haddock fillets, cut into 1-inch chunks
2 cups fresh corn, or 1 package (10 ounces) frozen corn, thawed
~~2 cups~~ milk *(1 c. milk)*
¼ cup chopped fresh dill

1. In a large saucepan, melt butter over medium heat. Add carrots, onion, and celery; sauté for 10 minutes, or until tender.

2. Stir in the clam juice, water, salt, cayenne pepper, and nutmeg; simmer for 10 minutes. Add the fish and corn and cook 10 minutes longer. Stir in milk and heat just to simmer. Spoon into serving bowls and sprinkle with dill.

SNAPPER IN CREAMY MUSTARD SAUCE

3–4 servings

2 tablespoons butter
¼ cup finely chopped onion
2 tablespoons white wine vinegar
¾ cup heavy cream
1 pound snapper, sole, or flounder fillets
1 tablespoon Dijon-style mustard
⅛ teaspoon freshly ground white pepper

1. In a large heavy skillet, melt butter over medium-low heat. Add onion and sauté for 10 minutes, or until very tender.

2. Raise heat to medium. Add the vinegar and boil until most of the liquid evaporates, about 1 minute. Add the cream and simmer until thickened and reduced, about 1 minute. Add the fillets, cover, and cook 2 to 3 minutes. With a slotted spatula, transfer fillets to a warm serving dish. Cover and keep warm.

3. Stir mustard and pepper into sauce and heat briefly, but do not boil. Spoon sauce over fish and serve.

SALMON, LEEK, AND MUSHROOM CHOWDER

"Chowders are homey fare, no matter how distinguished their ingredients," wrote M. F. K. Fisher in *With Bold Knife and Fork*. Try this rich and elegant chowder and see if you agree.

4–6 servings

2 tablespoons butter
1 large leek, thinly sliced   *or gr. onions*
1 cup dry white wine
3 potatoes (about 1 pound), peeled and cut
       into ½-inch pieces
8 ounces mushrooms, sliced
2 cups water   *no water*
1 bottle (8 ounces) clam juice   *or 4 gr. clams*
2 cups heavy cream   *(1)*
1 cup milk   *½*
¼ cup chopped fresh basil
1 pound skinless salmon fillet, cut into
       ½-inch pieces   *or trout*
¼ teaspoon white pepper
Salt to taste

1. In a large heavy saucepan, melt the butter over medium-low heat. Add the leek and sauté for 10 minutes.

2. Add the wine and simmer for 5 minutes. Add the potatoes, mushrooms, water, and clam juice; simmer for 20 minutes. Stir in the cream, milk, and basil. Return to simmer.

3. Add the salmon, pepper, and salt to taste. Cook just until salmon turns opaque, about 3 minutes.

MANHATTAN FISH CHOWDER

Like most soups, this chowder actually tastes better the day after it is made, once the flavors have had a chance to mellow and blend. Serve with oyster crackers and a big green salad.

6–8 servings

2 tablespoons olive oil
¼ pound sliced bacon, sliced into ½-inch pieces
2 cups chopped onions
4 carrots, chopped
2 celery stalks, thinly sliced
1 large green pepper, chopped
2 garlic cloves, minced
2 tablespoons chopped parsley
1 can (28 ounces) crushed tomatoes
1 bottle (8 ounces) clam juice
5 cups water
1 teaspoon dried thyme
1 bay leaf
2 teaspoons salt
¼ teaspoon black pepper
3 medium potatoes, cut into ½-inch cubes
1½ pounds cod, pollack, or ocean perch fillets, cut into 1-inch pieces

1. In a large saucepan, heat the olive oil and fry the bacon until almost crisp, about 5 minutes. Add the onions and sauté for 5 minutes. Stir in the carrots, celery, pepper, garlic, and parsley; sauté for 10 minutes more.

2. Stir in the tomatoes, clam juice, water, thyme, bay leaf, salt, and pepper. Bring to a simmer, reduce heat to low, cover, and cook for 45 minutes. Add potatoes and cook for 20 minutes. Add fish and cook for 5 minutes more.

SPAGHETTI with FISH, TOMATO, AND BLACK OLIVE SAUCE

4–6 servings

⅓ cup olive oil
1½ cups thinly sliced onions
1 can (28 ounces) Italian peeled tomatoes, chopped
2 large garlic cloves, finely chopped
1 teaspoon oregano
½ teaspoon salt
⅛ teaspoon pepper
Pinch red pepper flakes
¾ cup imported black olives, such as Kalamata, pitted and sliced
1 pound fish fillets, cut into 1-inch pieces
1 pound spaghetti
¼ cup chopped parsley

1. In a large saucepan, heat the oil over medium heat. Add the onions and sauté until tender, about 5 minutes. Stir in the tomatoes with their juice, garlic, oregano, salt, pepper, and red pepper flakes. Simmer for 20 minutes, or until thickened.

2. Stir in the olives and fish. Simmer for 3 minutes more.

3. Cook spaghetti until firm yet tender to the bite. Drain well and toss with sauce. Sprinkle with parsley and serve.

FETTUCCINE with SALMON, PEPPERS, AND PEAS

Pasta traditionally has been a good way to stretch a small amount of meat or fish. Here, the pink salmon, red peppers, and green peas in a creamy sauce are an appetizing combination over fresh fettuccine.

6 servings

2 medium red bell peppers
1 tablespoon butter
1 cup frozen tiny peas, thawed
1 cup heavy cream
8 ounces skinless salmon fillet or tuna steak, cut into ½ x ¼-inch pieces
½ teaspoon salt
⅛ teaspoon pepper
1 pound fresh fettuccine
¼ cup freshly grated Parmesan cheese

1. Preheat oven to 450°F. Lightly oil a small baking pan and bake the peppers for 25 minutes, turning occasionally, until evenly blistered. Place the peppers in a plastic bag and seal tightly. When cool, peel off pepper skins, and remove cores and seeds. Cut into ½-inch pieces.

2. In a large skillet, melt the butter over medium heat. Stir in the peppers and peas; sauté for 30 seconds. Add the heavy cream and bring to a simmer; cook, stirring frequently, until cream thickens, about 2 minutes. Stir in the salmon, salt, and pepper. Cook 1 minute.

3. Meanwhile, cook fettuccine in a large pot of boiling salted water until firm yet tender to the bite. Drain well, toss with sauce and Parmesan, and serve.

LINGUINE with MONKFISH AND FENNEL

Pasta with a Provençal touch of anchovies and fennel.

4–6 servings

¼ cup olive oil
1 cup chopped onions
2 large garlic cloves, chopped
1 green pepper, thinly sliced
1 can (2 ounces) flat anchovy fillets, chopped
    (reserve oil)
¼ to ½ teaspoon crushed red pepper
¼ teaspoon dried fennel seed
1 can (28 ounces) Italian peeled tomatoes,
    undrained and chopped
Salt and pepper to taste
1 pound monkfish or grouper fillets, cut into
    ¾-inch cubes
1 pound linguine

1. In a large saucepan, heat the oil over medium heat. Add the onions, garlic, green pepper, anchovies with their oil, red pepper, and fennel seed. Sauté for 10 minutes, or until vegetables are softened. Add the tomatoes and salt and pepper to taste. Bring to a boil, reduce heat, and simmer, stirring occasionally, for 15 to 20 minutes, until thickened.

2. Add fish. Cook 5 minutes more.

3. Cook linguine until tender yet firm to the bite. Drain well. Transfer to a large deep platter and spoon on the sauce.

CURRIED FISH

Curry powder is a blend of spices that varies greatly from one manufacturer to the next. Taste the sauce before adding the fish so you can adjust the seasoning.

4–6 servings

3 tablespoons butter
2 tablespoons curry powder
1 teaspoon ground coriander
1 teaspoon ground cumin
¼ teaspoon ground white pepper
Pinch cloves
Pinch cayenne pepper
Pinch nutmeg
1 teaspoon peeled and chopped fresh ginger-
    root
1 garlic clove, finely chopped
1 cup heavy cream
½ teaspoon salt
1½ pounds sole, snapper, or catfish fillets
Chopped roasted peanuts, raisins, and sliced
    scallions, for garnish

1. In a large skillet, melt the butter over low heat. Stir in the curry powder, coriander, cumin, pepper, cloves, cayenne pepper, nutmeg, gingerroot, and garlic. Cook, stirring constantly, for 2 minutes.

2. Stir in the cream and salt, raise heat to medium, and simmer for 1 minute, or until thickened.

3. Add fish. Cover and cook for 2 to 3 minutes.

4. Transfer fish to heated serving plates and spoon on sauce. Pass the peanuts, raisins, and scallions.

Sauces and Flavored Butters

"It's the sauce that makes the fish edible."
French Proverb

Most fish lovers agree that fresh fish needs little more than a squirt of fresh lemon juice to enhance its natural goodness. But a diet of plain broiled fish would quickly become monotonous. The following are some sauces and butter toppings that you might like to try on hot or cold fish that has been poached, grilled, or baked.

VEGETABLE-YOGURT SAUCE

A chunky, low-calorie sauce that's delicious on any poached or grilled fish.

Makes about 2 cups

1 cup plain low-fat yogurt
2 tablespoons chopped fresh mint
1 garlic clove, crushed
½ teaspoon ground cumin
½ teaspoon salt
¾ cup diced ripe avocado
½ cup diced seeded tomato
½ cup seeded cucumber
2 tablespoons finely chopped red onion

1. In a medium bowl, combine the yogurt, mint, garlic, cumin, and salt. Cover and refrigerate until serving time.

2. Stir in the avocado, tomato, cucumber, and onion. Serve immediately.

GREEN MAYONNAISE

The classic sauce for cold poached fish, especially salmon.

Makes about 1 ½ cups

¼ cup chopped spinach leaves
2 tablespoons chopped parsley
2 tablespoons chopped fresh tarragon or dill
2 tablespoons chopped chives or scallions
1 egg
¼ teaspoon dry mustard
¼ teaspoon salt
1 tablespoon lemon juice
1 ¼ cups light olive oil or salad oil

1. Bring 2 cups of water to the boil. Add the spinach and herbs. Cook for 2 minutes. Drain and run under cold water to stop the cooking. Drain well and pat with paper towels to remove excess moisture.

2. In a food processor or blender, combine the spinach mixture with the egg, mustard, and salt. Process until well blended. Add the lemon juice. With the machine running, add the oil a few drops at a time, until the sauce is thickened and all of the oil has been added. Cover and chill until serving time.

PESTO TARTAR SAUCE

Serve with fried fish or fish cakes.

Makes ¾ cup

¼ cup packed fresh basil leaves
1 large garlic clove
½ cup mayonnaise
¼ cup sour cream
1 teaspoon lemon juice
Dash hot pepper sauce

1. In a food processor or blender, finely chop the basil and garlic.

2. Blend in the remaining ingredients until smooth. Cover and refrigerate for several hours or overnight.

RED PEPPER SAUCE

Makes about 1 cup

3 red bell peppers (about 1 pound)
1 teaspoon vegetable oil
1 garlic clove, finely chopped
1 tablespoon chopped fresh basil, or
    ½ teaspoon dried
¼ cup heavy cream
1 tablespoon white wine vinegar
½ teaspoon sugar
½ teaspoon salt
White pepper to taste

1. Preheat the oven to 400°F. Rub the peppers with the oil and place them in an 8-inch square baking pan. Bake, turning occasionally, until the skin is blistered, about 30 minutes. Place the peppers in a plastic bag and seal tightly; let them stand until cool enough to handle.

2. Peel, seed, and cut the peppers into 1-inch strips. Transfer to a food processor; add the garlic, basil, cream, vinegar, sugar, salt, and pepper. Process until smooth. Transfer to a small saucepan and heat gently.

FLAVORED BUTTERS

Keep these tasty butters on hand in the freezer for a quick topping. To prepare, combine all the ingredients in a food processor or blender. Process or blend until smooth. Shape the butter into a 1-inch-thick log on a piece of plastic wrap. Wrap tightly and refrigerate or freeze. To use, slice off about ¼ inch for each serving of fish. Place on top of fish before baking or microwaving, or let soften at room temperature, then spread on hot steamed, poached, grilled, or broiled fish.

Olive Butter

1 cup imported black olives, such as
    Kalamata
1 stick (4 ounces) butter
1 garlic clove
Pinch pepper

Anchovy Butter

1 stick (4 ounces) butter
3 anchovy fillets
1 tablespoon Dijon-style mustard
1 garlic clove
Pinch cayenne pepper

Lime and Chili Butter

2 teaspoons grated lime peel
1 stick (4 ounces) butter
1 teaspoon chili powder

Jalapeño Butter

1 tablespoon finely chopped jalapeño or other
    hot chili
1 garlic clove
1 stick (4 ounces) butter

Index

California Blackened Snapper

1 Can (16 oz) peach halves, in syrup
1 Tbsp. paprika
2 tsp. salt
1 tsp. onion powder
1 tsp. garlic powder
3/4 tsp. white pepper
3/4 tsp. black pepper

1/2 tsp. cayenne pepper
1/2 tsp. thyme
1/2 tsp. oregano
6 red snapper fillets, about 1 1/2 lbs.
2 Tbsp. butter

Drain peaches reserving all liquid. Combine paprika with salt, onion powder, garlic powder, white, black and cayenne peppers, thyme and oregano. Mix well. Dip fish in peach liquid. Sprinkle both sides with paprika mixture. Heat a 10" skillet on high for 5 min. Carefully add half the fish. Cut butter in small pieces and add half to skillet. Skillet will smoke as butter is added. Cook about 1 1/2 to 2 min. on each side or until fish flakes easily with a fork. Repeat with remaining fish. Fan peach halves over fish to serve.

6 servings.